Rise of the Emergency Manager:

Restructuring Emergency Services During a Time of Civil Unrest

Brian K. Rand

ISBN: 978-0-578-83656-0

DEDICATION

My wife Danielle is a true inspiration and patriot; her dedication to public service and the American people knows no end. Thank you for supporting our journey together and continuing to contribute all we can to a country that we love and cherish.

And to the American People, you are what makes defending this country an honor and a privilege.

★★★★

Contents

Acknowledgments

The United States Intelligence Community (IC.) | Pinkerton® Corporate Risk Management | The Metro Boston Watertown Fire Department | Peter Flynn - Paragon Graphic Design | The Boston Globe | Yahoo News | The New York Times | Senator Steve Scalise | Fox News | Tucker Carlson | CNN News | Reuters | The United States Marine Corps | The United States Army | 1st Fleet Antiterrorism Security Team Company (FAST Co.) | Dr. Janie Gittleman - Defense Intelligence Agency (D.I.A.) | Douglas Huffman – Office of the Director of National Intelligence (O.D.N.I.) | Craig Fugate, former Administrator of FEMA. | Target® Corporation | Carol McMahon, MA-CEM, M.E.P., N.E.M.A.A. | | My Boss and Friend: Col. Maynard Austin, C.O. U.S. Army Special Operations Command, Operational Detachment – Delta, CIA/DIA (Deceased) | The Cities of Boston and Watertown, MA | Anna Maria College | Salem State College | Middlesex Community College | College of the Albemarle | Sean Delaney, Esq. | Mom & Dad & Sharon | Defense Counterintelligence and Security Agency

INTRODUCTION

Emergencies are a part of life. No one is exempt or spared from how, where, or when an emergency or crisis will occur. The range of emergencies from personal, family, city-wide to global is on-going, changing, and more widespread today than ever before. On a national scale, we have seen recent events and emergencies act as a medium to propel domestic terrorist groups, such as Antifa. These groups create a myriad of social justice movements and extremism acts, which have caused massive civil unrest, decimating communities, and putting the public's health and safety in jeopardy. And still, other emergencies—like the novel coronavirus pandemic—seem to have an unlimited and nonprejudicial reach. As of July 2020, 188 countries worldwide are reported to have experienced COVID-19 cases. Regardless of the high degree of attention given to it, the pandemic rages forward. [1] And that is just what is happening now.

The nature of the emergency is that it is unplanned and unforeseen. Often there is an insufficient warning, as history has shown, in knowing when or where there will be a virus outbreak, civil unrest, looting, rioting, an earthquake, or other unpredictable events that can threaten the financial stability of a single business or a global economy. The response to emergencies requires urgency, swift action, and internalized processes with detailed steps to deal with such a crisis. Not only do emergencies pose an immediate threat to our environment, property, health, and our lives, but the mishandling of emergency responses can quickly turn situations exponentially worse.

★★★★

What Is an Emergency Manager?

While an emergency manager is, by definition, a single individual, the immense responsibilities they oversee appear to encompass duties of all public safety department leaders, including the police chief, fire department chief, head of the department of public works, and the mayor. Let's start with an example of why that is a fair statement: the coordination and mobilization of resources and efforts. [2] Resources can be anything from supplies to shelter, to transportation and equipment, to personnel. With many types and levels of emergencies, communities, cities, or states may run out of the necessary equipment and manpower required to manage the emergency at hand. An effective emergency manager may not initially have all the answers but is willing to ask questions and find the best solutions.

Although emergencies are, to a degree, surprising in nature, the *ultimate* emergency manager will be able to recognize when a disaster might strike. This kind of foresight is invaluable, especially when impending danger looms over citizens within the jurisdiction to be protected. Effective emergency managers will understand that there are ways to diminish the effects and impact emergencies can create and, at the very least, avoid the disaster as much as possible or minimize the damage done. This technique is known as "mitigation," and I will discuss this in later chapters. Mitigation is a term not all officials are familiar with or understand, as I have heard it misused time and time again.

Good emergency managers will have the ability to decipher whether incidents can be solved in simple steps, present a more complicated nature, or are just purely complex in both size and scope. Mistaking one situation for another can lead to a misallocation of valuable resources, including energy and time, and unnecessary risk to individuals. *Capable* emergency managers will assess the risks associated with emergencies, make agile decisions, distinguish the complexity level, and act accordingly. [3] For all incidents to be resolved, or regardless of the emergency manager's level of ability, following a systematic problem-solving process involving strong and collaborative networks will be essential to minimize the output given for an efficiently resolved issue.

Emergency managers also coordinate and develop situation reports on an on-going basis. As conditions change and new information is received at any minute during a precarious event, the task of adapting and handling critical information becomes tricky, and opportunities for errors increase exponentially. Updates that are accurate and dispersed to all the relevant parties must be done promptly. Amidst this process, the emergency manager will need to excel not only with difficulties such as functioning with interoperability between various outside agencies but also in building positive relations with personnel, partner agencies, the public, as well as those in traditional or social media and various sects of population-specific to their areas. Everyone in the information exchange circle will depend on the emergency manager's transparency, direction, and information. This extends to the masses often, and it is always crucial—at any scale—to get it right.

★ ★ ★ ★

Emergency managers are tasked with monitoring communities and sharing emergency preparedness information to minimize disasters' potential unfortunate impact. They are also tasked with protecting and preserving the citizens in the regions they watch over and giving people the chance to participate as volunteer responders. [4] The volunteers, who undergo reliable training programs offered by the Federal Emergency Management Agency (FEMA), state agencies, local governments, or private organizations like the Red Cross, can reduce the burden placed upon professional responders, which are often short-staffed. Emergency managers proactively take steps to raise community awareness while offering citizens opportunities to make a genuine difference in helping others in their community and protecting their own families and businesses at the same time.

And within an emergency management department and its personnel, preparedness stems from advantageous, useful, and up-to-date training programs. Individuals and public services that fall under the umbrella of emergency response—including first responders such as EMTs, police officers, and firefighters—not only prepare by participating in on-going training and exercises, but these activities include testing equipment, conducting emergency drills, monitoring situations, and even figuring out ways to prevent potential disasters from occurring through open communication with members of the public. Staying open to improvements within programs is critical and regular evaluation of them is gainful, as well. Emergency staff follows the emergency manager's lead in building rapport with community agencies since, without thriving partnerships and community "buy-in," limitations and failure are inevitable.

★★★★

Even after emergency events conclude, emergency managers and their teams are still on the scene, helping to restore and repair infrastructure and see that locations return to their original state or identify programs and funds available to help achieve that goal. [5] After disaster strikes, several victims can be left confused and lost, especially those who are elderly or members of special populations requiring assistance to accomplish simple daily tasks. Some will lose their loved ones, homes, or personal property, and others will lose their only financial means of employment. To aid those directly affected by emergency disasters, the emergency manager must now make decisions to prevent new issues from arising and assist with meeting the needs of those who are left struggling from the disaster's effects.

As the title would indicate, emergency managers prepare plans and procedures [6] to help lead and appropriately guide the response during incidents and the recovery after emergencies of different scales. While most emergency management *"specialists"* or *"technicians"* work directly for governments, others work for private companies or institutions such as hospitals and universities.

However, as you can see, the emergency manager's role is slightly different and should not be confused with other jobs containing "emergency" in their title. In this book, I am attempting to focus on the separation and understanding of the actual, single-entity emergency manager. This position requires excellent management capabilities, but it also requires very high leadership and training and high-level, independent decision-making. The ideal emergency manager will also have excellent cultural awareness since disaster can reach all citizens' communities, regardless of their background, race, or religion.

The best emergency managers will have a firm grasp of substantive and technical knowledge to know what and when to apply critical emergency practices and know their limitations. And finally, but not conclusively, good emergency managers will have professionalism, even under extreme stress and time constraints, and demonstrate assertive, ethical behavior [7]. The emergency manager can positively or detrimentally influence the response to emergencies in how hundreds of decisions are made and the accessibility and readiness of the personnel and networks they are partnered with.

★★★★

WHY AN EMERGENCY MANAGER IS THE RIGHT ANSWER:

Here are several key reasons why the emergency manager is the right answer to fill voids and lead the forefront of restructuring emergency services today and in the future.

Emergency Managers:

1. Provide cohesion and clarity in emergency services roles across the board by leading public safety in its entirety.

2. Are always aware of issues, updates, and challenges across all departments.

3. Help alleviate or remove the ego and power struggle of individual departments that may compete against each other in the emergency services hierarchy.

4. Prepare for *all* emergencies, not just fire emergencies or police emergencies.

5. Create a standard operational procedure and pictures for everyone to follow.

6. Involve community programs and volunteers into the more prominent, overall picture of success.

7. Achieve greater buy-in from city management and the community, as they are a direct liaison between the two.

8. Possess a greater depth of knowledge in the preparedness, mitigation, and resiliency of the community.

9. Focused on community-based solutions, such as training groups of community volunteers and ensuring all volunteers are vetted, background checked, and prepared.

10. Provide the best option and best practices to appropriately fill the void created if police departments are defunded or disbanded.

As the role of an emergency manager is in dire need of a reboot and upgrade in 2021, my vision and goals are to clarify this role, to show how it was under-utilized in the past and how to capitalize on it moving forward, and to share innovative and life-saving practices which have shown to be highly effective in emergency management cases across the U.S.

In chapter one, I would like to first look into common issues and misconceptions about emergency management, ranging from those in politics, the public, or various media outlets, to those who are building a career working in the emergency management field today.

★★★★

Common Unresolved Issues

As an evolving discipline, the *best* emergency managers will have a progressive mindset and be "politically agnostic." [8] In other words, they should be realists in dealing with a situation or event, regardless of their political influence or which party line they lean toward. Our job is to protect the masses, not the careers of politicians. Many emergency manager roles have new and expanding responsibilities and requirements to meet. When individual emergency managers are simply experts in one specific subject or field—such as natural disaster preparedness—this limitation can severely hamper their overall work scope. The unifying role that the emergency manager fulfills requires that this person excels at coordinating multiple agencies and managing dynamic, ever-changing information sources continuously.

★★★★

While having experience and wisdom is indispensable, I cannot understate how education can be a massive advantage in this field. The entry-level education required to be an emergency manager is not defined. However, you need to be a consummate professional and a *perpetual learner*.

Whatever path you choose, stay ahead of the latest trends and gain experience and advanced training. It is needed to expand your knowledge in a wide variety of specific field areas. After 20 years of emergency service, I continued to grow my expertise through professional state and federal training. First, obtaining an associate's degree in Fire Protection and Safety Technology to establish a solid foundation. Then, I completed a bachelor's degree in Fire Science Administration to deepen my administrative understanding and competence in this specialized area. But to broaden my aptitude and potential for successfully interacting with top-level leadership, as you will see is essential to success, I decided to study further and receive a master's degree in Public Administration and

Emergency Management (MPA-EM). Having gone through these academic years undoubtedly led to building a stable and robust foundation of my outlook into different aspects of emergency management and the specific sectors it included. But as one veteran firefighter once said to me, "I have never seen a book put out a fire," and that is where gaining real-life experience comes in.

★★★★

Gaining Experience the Hard Way: Two Multiple Alarm Fires in One Day

February 11, 2011 – Mutual Aid, Watertown, 3rd Alarm. Box 213, 27 Pequossette Street. Watertown special called Rescue 1 (with the Tactical Rescue for Air Supply), Squad 4 and Division 2 to fire on Second alarm. Companies assisted on defensive attack after command had called for building evacuation. Engine 9 responded to the fire on 3rd alarm and supplied a feeder line to the Watertown ladder truck. CambridgeEngine 5 covered Watertown Engine 2 on the 3rd Alarm.

February 11, 2011 - Mutual Aid, Watertown, 3rd Alarm. Box 318, 131 Boylston Street -Engine 5, Rescue 1, and Squad 4 to a second fire in Watertown. Fire through roof on arrival. Engine 5

I did not begin my career in the emergency management field. Instead, I first became a U.S. Marine Infantry Sergeant, serving and deploying to combat theaters with the U.S.M.C. 1st Fleet Antiterrorism Security Team Company (FAST Co.) stationed in Norfolk, VA. I then moved into fire protection services as a firefighter/EMT and then, over the years, progressed to various roles as a Fire Officer for the Metro Boston Watertown Fire Department. You may recognize Watertown's name from the movie *Patriot's Day,* which portrayed the city's role in the

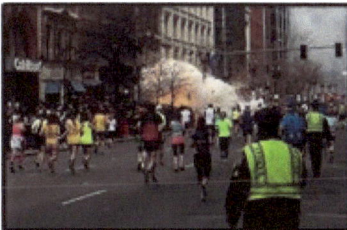
Photo credit: Boston Globe; web 2014

Photo credit: Boston Globe; web 2014

Photo credit: Boston Globe; web 2014

Photo credit: Boston Globe; web 2014

Boston Marathon Bombing and subsequent shootout with officers and the bombing suspects.

Photo credit: Boston Globe; web 2014

Innocence Lost: Martin Richard (8) Krystal Campbell (29) Lu Lingzi (23) Officer Sean Collier (27)

Photo credit: Boston Globe; web 2014
Watertown Police Officers Heroes Honored: (Pictured Left to Right) Officer Joseph Reynolds, Sgt. John MacLellan, and Sgt. Jeff Pugliese

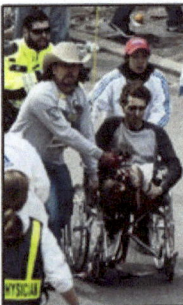

Photo credit: Boston Globe; web 2014

Wounded Amputee, Jeff Bauman With Carlos Arredondo

Photo credit: Boston Globe; web 2014

Boston Police Officer, Dennis Simmonds, Died of lasting wounds sustained from a grenade During the Watertown, MA Shootout

Photo credit: Boston Globe; web 2014
Officer Dick Donahue; wounded during shootout

I had the opportunity to move into specialized roles such as the Department of Emergency Medical Services (EMS) Coordinator, a Department Training Officer, Center for Disease Control (CDC) Certified Infection Control Officer, and finally, the Emergency Management Coordinator. During those years, I reenlisted and served as a U.S. Army Combat Medic and saw, firsthand, the devastation that the weapons of war can deliver to the unfortunate few. I was working on 9/11, and I remember it as though it was yesterday.

I will never forget.

★★★★

As I write this book, I need to highlight outdated ways of thinking, old-fashioned concepts, strengthening, enhancing, and replacing these plans with newer ones. Another major issue I have faced is 'group think,' which is an internal issue that arises in groups that prevent individuals from expressing their own opinions, thoughts, or concerns. I discuss this in later chapters on group dynamics and the social challenges of working with them. Many individuals and departments cling to obsolete methodologies for innovating and creating a better one to use. I also want to expose mismanagement, lack of understanding, and poor use of resources as common on-going problems occurring within the scope of an emergency manager's activities and influence.

★★★★

Often running parallel to these mishaps are poor decision-making processes and groupthink attitudes projecting, "it is already too late," to make any improvements or corrections when an emergency or disaster occurs. The emergency manager must be adequately and effectively-prepared to manage an emergency, regardless of the size, scope, or nature of the event. In fact, it is *literally* the job title. As the position of emergency manager continues to transform and duties rapidly expand, I want to share what has changed—or, more to the point—what has *not* changed at all. I have witnessed and experienced these issues firsthand over 20 years of public safety and emergency management roles in public service and private endeavors. Surprisingly, they all have the same unaddressed issues.

After I retired from the fire department, I became an emergency manager designated as a Subject Matter Expert (SME) in Chemical, Biological, Radiological, Nuclear, and High-Yield Explosions (CBRNE) for an intelligence agency within the Department of Defense and the United States Intelligence Community (IC). I specialized in the protection of the federal employees and contractors by studying seized data from the battlefield and reconstructing improvised explosive devices (IEDs) to test the efficacy and knowledge of the enemies of the United States and what these devices were capable of imposing on our troops and personnel in the homeland and various countries— specifically, ISIS and the Middle East.

After leaving government service, I remained a contracted advisor to the IC. for mass casualty planning for IEDs, active shooters, and other various large-scale incident responses, mitigations, and protection issues across the Intelligence Community and the Department of Defense.

This crucial previous experience led to becoming the Director of Pinkerton© Corporate Risk Management's Washington D.C., Maryland, Delaware, and Philadelphia Field Offices. It was here I was tasked to provide complete risk management strategies and private security services to the private sector—and what we will call "fringe" government activities—for over 90-percent of the Fortune 1000 companies and various U.S. government interests—such as the "off-campus" activities of the United States Congress. Pinkerton has a long and distinguished history of protecting high-profile individuals, dating back over 100 years. In fact, Pinkerton thwarted an assassination attempt on President Abraham Lincoln before there was such a thing as the United States Secret Service. Ever wonder who protects the CEOs and presidents of private companies around the world? That's right: America's oldest private detective agency, Pinkerton®. Pinkerton's company motto is "We Never Sleep," and I can fully attest to that motto standing true. They are fully operational, 24 hours a day, in over 100 countries worldwide. Their operational tempo is fast, precise, and exceptionally organized for such a large global footprint. It was not uncommon for a CEO, company president, or a global corporation's security department to call for services at three in the morning and need multiple armored vehicles, armed drivers, security personnel, and a global positioning system (G.P.S.) tracker in case of a kidnapping, all within the next hour, for they were leaving on a last-minute trip to Juarez, Mexico, or Hong Kong, China, or Panama, or the global location of their company's emergency.

WALKING IN THE FOOTSTEPS OF EXCEPTIONAL LEADERSHIP PRODUCES EXCEPTIONAL RESULTS.

Allan Pinkerton (Left) With President Abraham Lincoln.

My Boss and Friend, Col. Maynard Austin Laid to Rest at Arlington National Cemetery

My Chief and Friend, Mario Orangio LOD Due to Pancreatic Cancer

My Friend, Brother and Mentor, 1st Sgt. Kenneth Crutcher

A True Leader in Emergency Management and Friend and the Woman Who Knows It All, Carol McMahon, MA-CEM, MEP

A Great Man and Humanitarian, Sean Delaney, ESQ. Sean Turned My Life Right, When I was Heading Left as a Child

A Guardian Angel, Lin Ryan, RN Has Kept me "In Check" For over 25 Years

Two War Veteran and 27 Year Retired Army Master Sergeant, my Father Ken Rand

★★★★

Pinkerton® Through the Years: Then and Now

Pinkerton Badge and
Credentials (Circa 1920)

Pinkerton Badge and
Credentials (Circa 2017)

Pinkerton Logo (Circa 1920)

Pinkerton Logo (Circa 2016)

I was fortunate to hold these various positions throughout my professional career. I have dealt with municipalities, the federal government, private business executives, and agency leaderships—including directors, CEOs, military generals, state officials, local government, and county elected leadership. Through these professional relationships, I discovered the same issues consistently occurring no matter which location or group of people I encountered.

★★★★

When I completed audits of their security, emergency preparedness programs, and protocols, the ugly truth of the matter was uncovered and presented to the leadership—and that's when sparks began to fly. Put merely, deficiencies were identified, and the finger-pointing began. Immediately the respective individuals in charge no longer sought to be associated with the findings. They knew someone needed to be held accountable, and it was not going to be them. Any attempt to "put a band-aid on a bullet hole" was nothing more than basic damage control tactics for the sake of their career or political aspirations, not for the ethical or moral reasons of actually fixing the problems. In addition to this, the leadership typically asked me the same questions, in fancier terms: "What can we do with the least amount of money?" "What can we do to receive the least amount of bad publicity?" And one of my least favorites, "What are the options to disassociate from the problems completely?" The leadership often looked for shortcuts and resolutions that required the least amount of effort, exposure, and money. They'd ask me to point them in the direction of the path of least resistance and show them the ways that were most convenient or personally advantageous for them. It was my duty to not waiver from my recommendations, and sometimes, that was to my detriment. On more than one occasion, I was told, *"Maybe your pencil shouldn't be so sharp."*

★★★★

But enough about me. It would help if you saw where my credibility and experience are derived from. I'm actually a pretty humble guy who would be happy to speak with any of you about anything—especially your trials and tribulations in this field—but also in life in general. I have learned more from talking with people over the years that cannot, nor would ever, be found in a book. The door is always open. Enjoy the Book!

CHAPTER 1

THE PSYCHOMETRIC PARADIGM

I spoke briefly on expanding your education and experience, and the Psychometric Paradigm (pronounced para-dime) is just one of the many reasons I found continuing education so important. The "Psychometric Paradigm"—developed by Paul Slovic (pictured below left), Baruch Fischhoff, and Sarah Lichtenstein (pictured below right)— were a bedrock in research about public attitudes toward perceived risks. In simple terms, they asked, "are you afraid of it or not? And if so, why?"

Paul Slovic, professor of psychology at the University of Oregon and the president of Decision Research

Sarah Lichtenstein, co-founder of Decision Research contributed to the creation of : the Society of Judgment and Decision Making

The theory compared the experience of professionals in the field of risk management to the opinions and attitudes of the general public. This paradigm theory produced a "cognitive map" of hazards and described how the two groups perceived the same topic or situation's danger (risk). Without going 'too far down a rabbit hole,' the paradigm's basic theory is that experts can and will foresee or interpret risk based on their experience. Conversely, the layperson's attitude toward the same situation is established by how afraid they are and the likelihood of it happening.

★★★★

For example, if a fire alarm goes off in an apartment building, we can safely assume that both parties know that a fire is deadly. A majority of laypersons understand that there

High-rise fire victims: 'False alarms were routine'
Fire officials have also revised the tally of injured residents, raising it to at least 18

SAN ANTONIO — Two of five people who died Sunday morning in a fire at a senior living high-rise in Castle Hills have been identified.

According to the Bexar County Medical Examiner, Jose O. Gonzales, 73, and Karen Rae Betz, 74, died around 6 a.m. when a fire gutted at least one floor of the 11-story Wedgwood Senior Living apartments in the 6700 block of Blanco Road.

Story Credit: Dec 30, 2014
San Antonio Express-News

may or may not be a fire when the fire alarm goes off. Some will exit the building as a precaution, some may wait to see fire or smoke, and some individuals may not leave at all. This response depends on how each person perceives the risk *individually*. If they feel afraid, they will act accordingly.

The theory then suggests that professionals calculate risk differently. When a fire alarm goes off, they take all of the available information at hand and decide based on the facts presented and their experience. But what does that mean? It means that the expert will process the facts. Fact: An alarm gave a warning. "What floor am I on, and how long will it take me to reach safety," "If I leave first before there is confirmation of a fire, will my chances increase of avoiding the crowd rushing to the exits," "How much energy will I expend leaving now vs. waiting," "What are the available exit routes and which one is the quickest vs. the safest" "Do any other factors influence my decision to exit the building regardless of if there is, or is not a fire." By calculating the risk percentage, the benefits of exiting outweigh the benefits of staying and is therefore worth the perceived inconvenience of exiting, regardless of a fire or not.

Firefighters rely on the fire alarm to produce a specific universal result and hope that the public will always react accordingly. However, according to the Psychometric Paradigm theory, when a fire alarm **continuously** goes off, the public perception of risk lowers and eventually leads to **no** perceived risk, meaning no one will leave if the fire alarm activates again and again. The alarm is no longer perceived as a warning but instead as a nuisance.

Elmira, NY Fire Department File Photo

"Complacency is not good at all and it does occur. You get buildings that have alarm systems and (residents) tend to ignore it, and that can have some pretty big price tags," he said. "Suddenly here's the real deal. People need to react. There are times when it's routine and not a big deal, but other times it is. Our job is getting people to be mindful and pay attention, be looking for signs of something more serious."

- Retired Elmira, NY Fire Chief, Patrick Birmingham

★ ★ ★ ★

The Psychometric Paradigm is an essential concept of understanding human nature and how it directly affects emergency management and public safety thinking and planning. The more the government enacts drastic

Photo credit: dailymail.co.uk "3994640" Richard Reid (Shoe bomber) (web, 2020)

measures or imposes a hypothetical inconvenience for the sake of "public safety" for an event that has not *actually* happened, the public loses confidence in their ability to predict risk correctly. This is especially important to understand and grasp because the next time a warning is given about a perceived risk from "experts," the public will not have the same reaction, and the impact of their trust will be diminished over time. Think about the last time you went to the airport, and people were upset about taking off their shoes at the security checkpoint. Many young public individuals probably don't remember Richard Reid, the *"Shoe Bomber,"* a British terrorist who attempted to detonate a shoe bomb while on American Airlines Flight 63 from Paris to Miami in 2001.

Reid converted to Islam as a young man in prison after years as a petty criminal. Later, he became radicalized and went to Pakistan and Afghanistan, where he trained and became a member of al-Qaeda.

★★★★

The Event:

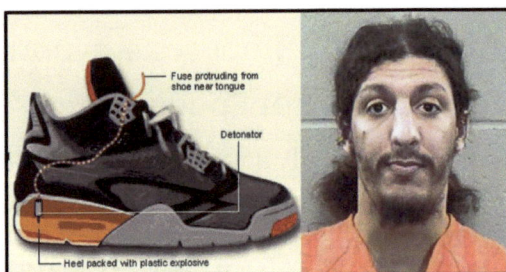

Photo credit: dailymail.co.uk "3994640" Richard Reid (Shoe bomber) (web, 2020)

In 1995, Reid was released from prison, and he embraced Islam, changing his name to Abdel Rahim. Initially, his conversion seemed a positive step, and Reid stayed out of trouble. By late 1997, however, he had apparently fallen in with a more radical group. Reid became more vociferous and militant in his views, reportedly becoming

estranged from family members who would not convert to Islam. In December 2001, he returned to Europe, flying to Brussels, and obtained a new British passport in an apparent attempt to conceal his recent travels. Later in December, Reid purchased an expensive pair of basketball shoes with cash and then took a train to Paris, where he bought a round-trip plane ticket in cash to Antigua that stopped in Miami. Reid was scheduled to leave on December 21st, 2001, but his cash purchase of the plane ticket, his agitated state, and the absence of luggage triggered an extensive security check at the airport. He missed the flight. That evening, he went to an Internet café and sent an e-mail to someone in Pakistan, asking for advice. His correspondent instructed him to try again, and the next day, he successfully boarded American Airlines Flight 63, flying from Paris to Miami. About 90 minutes after the plane took off, a flight attendant smelled sulfur and realized that Reid had lit a match. She made him put it out, but he lit another and attempted to set fire to the tongues of his shoes. When she intervened, Reid attacked her, knocked her down, and then bit another attendant. Passengers quickly responded, holding Reid down, tying him up with belts and cords, and dousing him with water. A doctor on board eventually injected him with sedatives. The flight landed at Logan International Airport in Boston, Massachusetts, the closest U.S. airport. He was arrested, charged, and indicted. In 2002, Reid pleaded guilty in U.S. federal court to eight federal criminal counts of terrorism, based on his attempt to destroy a commercial aircraft in flight. He was sentenced to three life terms, plus 110 years in prison, without parole, and was transferred to A.D.X. Florence, a super maximum-security prison in Colorado. [9]

★★★★

After Senator Steve Scalise was shot during an annual softball game in Alexandria, Virginia, in 2017, I was brought in to complete a detailed security study and analysis to identify and resolve protection issues for congressional members engaging in

Photo credit: noia.org "noia-annual-meeting"
Spearker/Congressman-Steve-Scalise (web; 2020)

activities off the capitol grounds. These were situations like fundraising events, social gatherings and dinners, and international travel for the congressmen and women and their families. You may or may not know (it was even a surprise to me), but only certain congress members receive police protection once they step off the U.S. House and Senate grounds. These unprotected members of congress were scared, and rightfully so after the senator was shot.

The shooter:
James T. Hodgkinson, 66, opens fire with a military-style rifle on lawmakers, staffers and Capitol Police before being shot. He died later at an area hospital.

EUGENE SIMPSON STADIUM PARK
ALEXANDRIA, VA.

Outfield

Steve Scalise:
The Republican Majority Whip from Metairie was shot in the hip and crawled toward the outfield. He was transported to an area hospital, underwent surgery and is listed in critical condition.

3rd base
2nd base
Dugout
1st base

David Bailey:
Capitol Police officer who was injured and limped out to Scalise to check on him after the shooter was taken down.

Zack Barth:
A staffer for U.S. Rep. Roger Williams, R-Texas, Barth was shot in the leg and limped off the field toward the dugout, where others had taken cover.

Dugout   Batting cage

Others injured: Krystal Griner, a Capitol Police officer, and Matt Mika, a lobbyist, were also injured during the attack.

Photo/Graphic credit: Dan Swenson, Graphics Editor • Animator | The Advocate & Times-Picayune (web 2020)

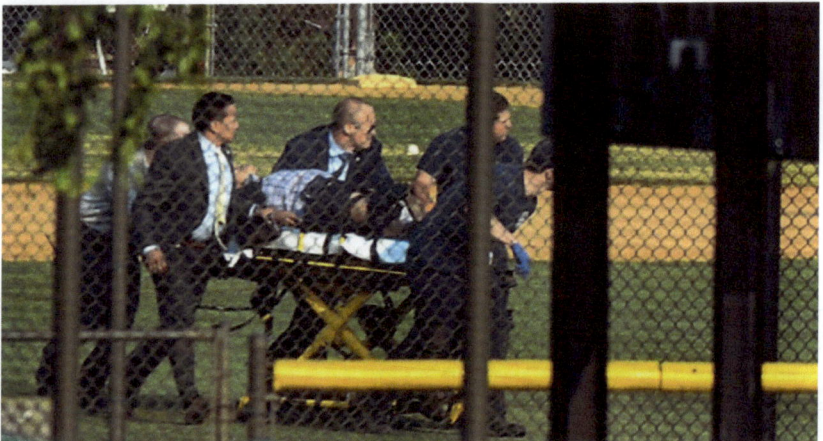

Photo credit: Washington Post, web 2020

★★★★

After completing this assignment, I presented the appropriate solutions for strengthening protection and security from bad actors who would want to hurt or injure politicians off the capitol's grounds. It turns out, the agency that hired me only wanted to show that they had taken decisive action via a comprehensive study to both ease fears and feign a show of concern—in essence, to check off a box—and wait out the panic. Imagine getting an estimate for your car brakes to be fixed, then deciding to take your chances with your current worn brake pads because you are too frugal to put long-term safety over the short-term cost.

When it came time to implement new strategies, the client ignored every solution strongly suggested for the safety of the politicians, constituency, and their families. They wanted to show they took action, without actually taking action – they got an estimate. And you know what? It worked like a charm – until the next time. Enter the presidential inauguration of Joe Biden, and the media proclaimed 'insurrection' of Capitol Hill. The short-term cost of enhanced security before the event was estimated at a one-time cost of $150,000 and an annual operating cost of $110,000 a year. The cost of mobilizing tens-of-thousands of national guard troops as an after-the-fact reaction is estimated at $2,600,000 a day.

Likewise, I was assigned to initiate and conduct a massive preparedness audit and create emergency management plans to be implemented for the Defense Intelligence Agency (D.I.A.) enterprise. As a subject matter expert., I spent the next six months reviewing, rewriting, and correcting an antiquated and incomplete plan. Similar to the abovementioned situation, when this audit was completed and a 150-page document was presented to the leadership, they were shocked, embarrassed, and angry at the findings. I could figuratively see them looking for a rock to crawl under as I went over page after page in great detail during a meeting with the agency's Senior Executive Service (S.E.S.) officers and their counterparts. You will see the term "operational gap" used in later chapters, and this was precisely what had occurred: years of mismanagement, misdirection, misuse of funds, false reports to the Director of National Intelligence (ODNI) about allotted billets for positions and capabilities, and half a million dollars' worth of chemical sensory equipment - that no one could account for or even heard of. As leadership came and went so quickly in the agency, one person's negligence became another's inheritance. Over time, a constant stream of inexperienced leadership with no operational experience created an operational gap, a period of time where the unit's operations were at a standstill as the issues compounded without resolution.

The report's revelations were so unsettling the leadership decided they would rather risk a disastrous event happening instead of facing the repercussions of being investigated due to the failures the audit exposed. Prioritizing their careers and upcoming promotions over preventing a potentially hazardous event toward the workforce showed the lack of professionalism and ethics. When a feeble attempt to hold an orchestrated exercise was conducted, all of the critical issues were either ignored, eliminated from the scenario, or were hidden by a phenomenon known as "theater"—which pretended the issue had already been dealt with. Like much of the public, they assumed other federal government agencies would magically swoop in and take care of all of their issues without ever testing that hypothesis or making a single phone call to see what their *actual* capabilities were.

Shakespeare himself could not have written a better playbill for the audience. It likened to North Korean Dictator, Kim Jong Ill, trying to show how advanced North Korea and its infrastructure were compared to the rest of the world. He used theater, controlled, prerecorded, and edited "interviews" complete with faked pictures, phony storefronts, and empty hotels. Reporters were preselected, accompanied by close armed guards posing as "tour guides."

I witnessed the sheer level of ignorance that indicated it was time for me to go, as I could not sit by and watch this continue with no resolution in sight and repercussions for it. So, I went onto greener pastures—or so I thought. And you know what? Again, it worked like a charm because nothing had happened, and therefore, they perceived no immediate risk. Except for the active shooter, Aaron Alexis, previously killing 12 people across the river at the Washington Navy Yard in 2013.

★★★★

The Impact of Massive Civil Unrest on the Public, Business Owners, and Cities Across the U.S.

In 2020, the world became witness to recent and massive civil unrest sweeping through the U.S., where the unrest was initially triggered. With the murder of George Floyd on May 25th, 2020, by a Minneapolis police officer came an upheaval of protests, riots, and petitions, including company position statements and changes unlike any other time in history. The simmering hotspots in many U.S. cities, which have experienced and continue to experience great injustices to its black community, have collided with old systems and placed this issue in the limelight—not only across our news stations but around the globe.

The response to this civil unrest seems not to be leaving any political or social stone unturned. Everyone—from rural cities to metropolises, and from America's largest corporations to its smallest businesses—is tuned into the message of changing the systems and structures as we've known them, and thousands of people are not backing down.

Especially amid the COVID-19 pandemic, it is unusual to see the rise of two incredibly significant events impacting most human beings on Earth at the same time. Millions of Americans have become unemployed, with the coronavirus death toll only moving upward. Halfway through 2020, we were in a time like no other, and it was by no means close to being over, and we knew it would continue for quite some time.

★★★★

Reduction of Response and Emergency Services

The collision of these events means expected public services are no longer certain. New environments, and public sentiment on defunding police services, in some cases, resulted in requests to reduce the response or activation of emergency services, mainly in the demand to defund police services in numerous communities. While this process can mean a reallocation of funds away from police departments and into communities in certain cities, it means a complete unguided dismantling and rebuilding phase with no definitive or logical plan to fill the void of the lost essential element of safety and security -- the missing cops.

These changes are instrumental to new environments; however, their efficacy is questionable, at best. New ideas are being planned and shaped in local communities, and the unknown is bringing up a lot of valid questions and concerns. Nevertheless, with the strong public sentiment and

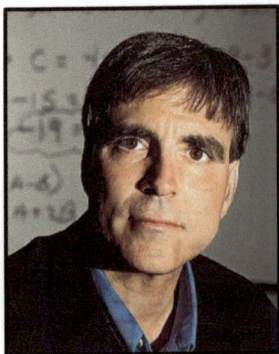

Katja Heinemann / Aurora Select / Courtesy of Parade Magazine

support of these changes, the traditional, publicly funded services integrated into our cities are now sitting upon the unsteady ground and no longer a shining city on a hill. As emergency managers, our attitudes must reflect the task at hand—unbiased, apolitical, indifferent, and ready to face the challenges head-on.

One phrase by Randy Pausch *(pictured above, left)* often comes to mind. As an inspirational speaker and technology juggernaut, he once said,

"*We can't change the hand we are dealt, just how we play the hand.*"

A poker game reference, indicating there is turmoil ahead, and we have to prepare for it, regardless of our personal feelings and opinions. We can fold, give up, do nothing, or play the hand as best we can, even though we may lose. This was good advice from a wise man who was tragically taken too soon by pancreatic cancer. But his words live on and are more accurate than ever today and moving forward.

CHAPTER 2

THE POWER VACUUM: FILLING THE VOID

Failed Public Attempts

Do citizens and politicians alike understand what they are asking for? What about the decisions made to defund law enforcement agencies blindly? How will they then change direction, operate on less funding, and re-train their staff to satisfy the public eye? With the pullback of the impact of emergency services in communities, the natural result will be an absence of what has now been removed: law and order. How this void will be filled is now the question. This can lead to uncertainty and the opportunity and likelihood that what fills its void is undesirable—or as with many examples in history, far worse.

The power vacuum created when Saddam Hussein was removed from power in Iraq in 2003 directly led to the creation, growth, and rise of the Islamic State in Syria (ISIS) and the subsequent Islamic State of Iraq and the Levant (ISIL), which took advantage of the massive grab for power left by the unplanned void of a ruthless dictator after he was removed from power with no replacement. The United States and its allies figured that removing an authoritarian leader would evolve into a new democracy for Iraq's people. It did not.

★★★★

In a recent example of disorder, Capitol Hill, a neighborhood in Seattle, Washington, known for its foodies,

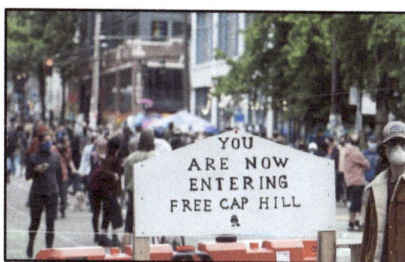
Photo Credit: Yahoo News (web 2020)

students, artists, sizeable alternative population, and fighters against gentrification—was filled with intense protests in early June of 2020 to promote and represent the Black Lives Matter movement.

Some of the protests became violent standoffs. [10] After days of thousands of loud protesters standing their ground outside the doors of one of Seattle's five police stations, the department decided to close up shop. More than 20 unvetted and possibly unlicensed volunteer "medics" and groups of internal security "goon squads" began serving those who became injured. Then they began serving as Capitol Hill security during these protests. Many declared Capitol Hill a cop-free zone.

As the police department barred its doors to the public, a makeshift street market called "no-cop co-op" developed, and several misbranded "peaceful" demonstrations in this area were now called Capitol Hill Occupied Protest (CHOP), which "intended to document or culturally preserve" the occupation. This name was later changed to Capitol Hill Autonomous Zone (CHAZ) to focus on its efforts on the organized protests it aimed to hold, or so they thought. [11]

The community started to draw homeless people from other parts of Seattle and began to settle there. CHAZ has

Photo credit: Yahoo News; (web; 2020)

been widely supported and also frowned upon, as the presence of policing activity had disappeared overnight. Many see this only as an act of rebellion, while others applaud the efforts in standing up for all those who've been sorely underrepresented and mistreated. But how will this community thrive in

AMERICA'S LEADERS: NOTHING TO SEE HERE
· TUCKER CARLSON tonight · #Tucker

"Countries Have Borders, and the Founders of CHAZ Understand That"

-Tucker Carlson, FOX News

Photo credit: nationalfile.com, Pappert, Tom (Editor-and-Chief) National file (web, 2020)

the absence of essential emergency support and monitoring? [12] Weeks later, reports began to surface of violence within CHAZ—a break-in into an auto shop [13], two occupant citizens being shot with one killed—and then, many protesters began moving out of the autonomous zone. [14] When other shootings transpired, and conditions began to deteriorate, the city decided they had no choice but to intervene and ask the protesters to now go home.

In this case, what filled the void was only the further threat of public health and safety jeopardy. There wasn't anything to take the place of the emergency services already present there. After several weeks and the avoidable murder of two *additional* young black men, CHAZ was officially called off. The irony of it all was that CHAZ created its borders, laws, immigration policy, and security forces with guns to enforce the rules. What does this resemble? These were the very issues they were protesting to be defunded and removed in the first place.

★★★★

CHAPTER 3

MISCONCEPTIONS OF EMERGENCY MANAGEMENT

The Difference Between an Emergency Manager and A Public Safety Commissioner

While some larger cities have a fire commissioner or a police commissioner in place as their chief officer, other cities have one person doing both or numerous jobs. This person is usually called a *public safety commissioner*. A public safety commissioner may be one individual in smaller towns—typically, a general administrator, such as a mayor or town manager—overseeing all the departments. Usually, you will see this in situations where a municipality needs to save money, and the departments are small and manageable. The title of fire commissioner or a police commissioner is an interchangeable term with the department's chief in larger communities or municipalities.

The difference between an emergency manager and a public safety commissioner is that a commissioner is the head of a specialized, singular department, such as the police or fire departments. They work together but do not influence the decisions for each separate department. An emergency manager, on the other hand, is an expert in all emergency fields. Known as, and even required to be, a jack of all trades, emergency managers understand how each department fits into the larger picture of total public safety, disaster preparedness, training, and community involvement. And even as police departments are becoming defunded and disbanded in some cities in the U.S. today, the instability this can create in some departments is already understood by an emergency manager, including what best steps to take next to compensate for this vacancy. This issue, along with other practical reasons, makes emergency managers' presence critical to cities' well-being today.

★★★★

Emergency Management Paradigm Shift

Emergency management (E.M.) is often not fully understood by department or agency leadership, including those in policing, fire, emergency medical services (EMS), as well as the Department of Public Works (DPW), etc. As each department prioritizes its goals and needs, it is accustomed to functioning and operating as its entity—independent from other departments. And rightly so, as each department has its focus and unique capabilities to offer to the public in times of disasters. However, when emergencies arise which require cooperation and partnership between several groups, many departments do not always see the need to take the lead from the emergency management team, even though emergency management is best designed to oversee all the departments in cases like these. Being free from having to specialize in one area or the other, the emergency management team is free to operate at its best when functioning as the lead in large crises.

Not recognizing the best place for emergency management to operate is the uncertainty of the ideal structure, allowing emergency management to lead. I can liken this to an example of baking a cake. Since most of us are probably more familiar with baking a cake than emergency management placement in an organizational structure, it will likely be a bit easier to understand. Here is a list of what is needed to make a cake, as follows: milk, eggs, sugar, baker, flour. Which item stands out as being different from the rest but is still essential to the cake is a success?

We would say that the **baker** is not an ingredient and does not belong in this category list. As important as having the baker create a cake, the baker is not an ingredient, but rather the actual person who facilitates and makes all the ingredients combine into a successful cake.

Checking off that you have all the ingredients in step one, just as making sure all the components and departments are available in various emergencies. The baker is key to baking this cake. However, being placed in the **wrong category** prevents the baker from doing their job appropriately, if at all. The baker will never produce the end product until you move the baker into the correct category: the architect to all of the ingredients coming together.

This analogy highlights the issue with emergency management. Since those in political leadership roles, such as mayors or elected officials, often do not have any experience in emergency services operations, they cannot comprehend the best way for an emergency manager to function; they lump it in with the other services and misuse it as a single additional service. But once the emergency manager, like the baker, is allowed to do their job correctly, managing all the ingredients in the recipe, cities will have their best chance to avoid a recipe of disaster. Pun intended.

★★★★

Right now, leadership typically has emergency management as just another extension of an existing department, usually a fire department. Leadership does not recognize that the answer to their issues is right under their nose. Once emergency management is categorized correctly and an emergency manager is set in place, emergency management becomes an invaluable asset and not only beneficial to everyone involved in emergencies but the public who they are ultimately called to serve and protect.

In certain cities, emergency management programs are often pushed to the side, or "pigeon-holed," into dealing with issues that other departments deem not worthy of their time and use of their budget—like natural disaster preparedness, pandemic preparedness, community programs, and serving on councils or working groups, etc.

After a year of new and progressing social challenges and widespread disorder, can you imagine what the overall situational picture looks like when everyone is unprepared, not on the same page, and not taking direction from emergency management, whose entire purpose is dedicated to resolving emergencies like the ones we are experiencing today? Well, let me tell you that it is precisely what is happening. For your informational purposes, I suggest you call your community leadership and ask what their overall management plan is to resolve any of the events we face today. Just watch your eyes when the finger-pointing starts.

★★★★

Three-legged Stool Failure

When the emergency manager is considered one part, or a single element of emergency response, rather than the actual leader for managing the emergency, it is a clear sign of management not understanding the emergency manager's role. When this happens, there is a misuse of a significant asset available to any sector that faces emergencies and needs the right form of leadership capability in place.

Emergency management works best when all the components or agencies involved in an emergency response fall under its umbrella of emergency management. Here is why: these components will usually include police, fire, emergency medical services, and other municipal services. When there are too many in charge, it is challenging to move numerous components toward the same goal. Depending on the type of incident, the other supporting departments' response is not always positive. This issue can be due to ego or a strong reluctance to resigning control during an event. These responses create a lack of unity and cohesiveness between the multiple departments and significantly limit what can be done to serve the public in times of great need. As George Gascoigne once said, "Without a conductor, every player has an idea for how the music should go; too many cooks spoil the broth." [15]

★★★★

As you will see in the diagram below, today's typical set-up has the existing elected leadership for the community placed as the stool's seat, thus overseeing the components, including the emergency manager. And when you remove one of the legs due to things like defunding, dismantling departments, or scarce resources, the stool immediately fails, and everyone fails with it.

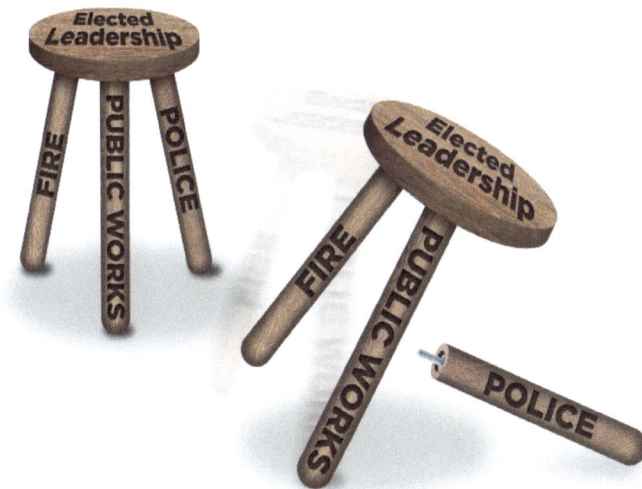

★★★★

Unfortunately, this happens when emergency managers are not given the go-ahead to take the lead. Things like the anticipation of disasters, preparedness, or cohesion across the board, which are among emergency management specialties, are shortsighted or overlooked. Thus, many communities and cities end up ill-prepared for such events. This is understandable since someone unfamiliar with leadership acting as the emergency manager is typically incapable or does not possess the essential skills for what the role requires. They are elected officials and often have no general knowledge of how the incident command structure (ICS) or the National Incident Management System (NIMS) works.

★★★★

Looking at the following diagram, this model is reflective of emergencies where the emergency manager is put in the right place. When correctly structured, even if one of the subsections falls off, the structure will still sound because the emergency manager maintains the balance and output needed while exercising its leadership. And when the emergency manager is not one of the legs or subsections, it can adequately serve as the main bridge for all the structural components. This not only allows emergency management to flourish in its skillfulness, but it also allows the leadership of the components to focus on their respective expertise and the individual department's mission and goals.

★★★★

During a fire, the fire chief should not be worried about what police officers' duties are. Additionally, during a fire scene, the police should not be focused on if the Department of Public Works is doing their job. That is why an emergency manager is so critical during emergencies. One primary goal is to support and free-up the operational components to do their job **without** distraction.

In comparison, a military unit encompasses a similar structure and placement of the company First Sergeant (1stSGT). The 1stSGT, serving as the top enlisted member of a unit, is comparable to the emergency manager's role in a command structure for emergency services. They don't *outrank* the officers in charge—such as the chiefs of a department or the platoon leaders/company commanders—but they do hold power to act on their behalf to allow them to focus on their particular leadership responsibilities, such as logistical and planning issues. The 1stSGT handles the daily operational hurdles and issues involving the individual enlisted members, such as disciplinary action, gear malfunctions, equipment issues, obtaining vehicles, etc.—just as the emergency manager handles any issues during an event, such as media, logistics, operational issues, and overall, operational, hands-on approaches that can prevent chiefs from supervising the safety of their members.

Incident Command: Who SHOULD Be in Charge and Why?

Why doesn't every city and state then simply appoint an emergency manager? As the administrative leadership structures differ from city to city and state to state, there will not always be an emergency manager or department in place. In fact, there may not be a full-time fire department in-place. Since disaster incidents must have a leader, regardless of administrative staff and departments' structure, *someone* will inevitably need to be in charge. In other words, according to Homeland Security Presidential Directive-5 (HSPD-5)'s National Incident Management System (NIMS) and Incident Command Structure (ICS), someone needs to *assume command*. But who should it be? If you are not familiar with either of the two above-listed directives, the answer may surprise you. If you are not familiar with either of the above-listed directives, it *probably* will not be you.

In larger-scale, local, emergency events, the leadership for the incident is stripped from a department chief and assumed by local government officials, regardless of how much training or experience they have and usually only when things are going right. I respectfully disagree with this practice. During an event, you really should have the most experienced individual or agency be in charge, regardless of rank, title, or authority.

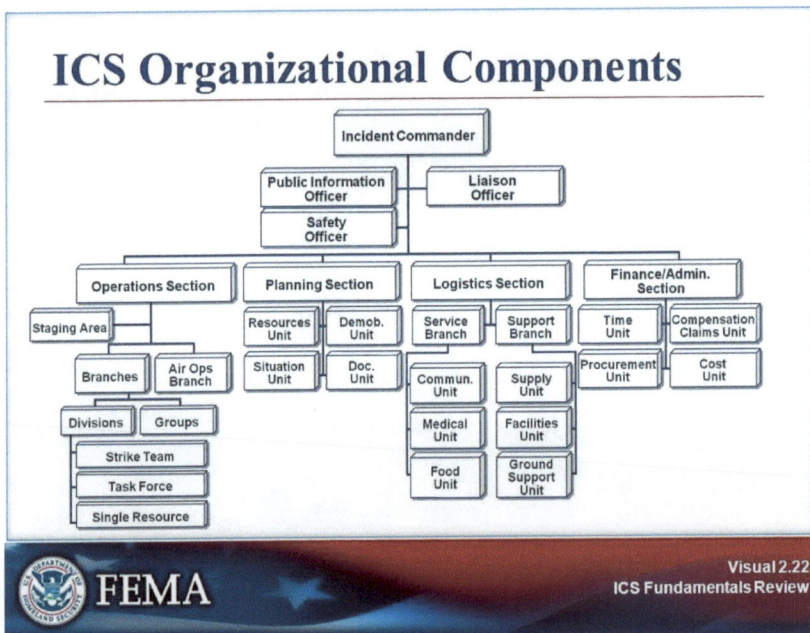

ICS Organizational Components

73

Knowledge and ability are beneficial to those first responders and the public who depend on services in their time of need. It's not only my professional opinion but listed in NIMS, as well. Don't believe me? It's in there.

Furthermore, did you know that the Incident commander can be more than one person at the same time? When utilizing a unified command, all independent agency heads can act as one incident commander jointly. Yes, that is in there too:

"Unified Command When no one jurisdiction, agency, or organization has primary authority and the resources to manage an incident on its own, Unified Command may be established. In Unified Command, there is no one "commander." Instead, the Unified Command manages the incident by jointly approved objectives. A Unified Command allows these participating organizations to set aside issues such as overlapping and competing authorities, jurisdictional boundaries, and resource ownership to focus on setting clear priorities and objectives for the incident. The resulting unity National Incident Management System 23 of effort allows the Unified Command to allocate resources regardless of ownership or location. Unified Command does not affect individual agency authority, responsibility, or accountability." [40]

When the state, federal, and other emergency response agencies respond to a crisis event, there needs to be a standardized communication system, command, and control. The Incident Command System (ICS)[16] is a standardized hierarchical system for agencies within and outside of government responding to an emergency.

Many people believe that NIMS and ICS came-to-be after the September 11th attack on the World Trade Center in 2001 due to the multiple agencies lacking a clear command structure for the response and the sheer scope size of the incident. That's not entirely true, and it's not entirely false. NIMS and ICS were developed almost 30 years prior in California during their intense wildfires in 1973. The forestry service and the fire departments began creating and applying the first version of NIMS in the 1970s. They had great success with resolving interoperability of communications, an ordinary working terminology, and eliminating redundant command orders from multiple chiefs from multiple districts. In the 1980s, it was widely accepted throughout California. It was given the California Governor's approval to be used at all jurisdictional levels, regardless of the incident's size. In 2003, President Bush wanted to adopt a national level of incident management (Homeland Security Presidential Directive-5) and incident command system to avoid future issues of mass-scale responses from multiple state and federal agencies not knowing who was in charge to communicate with each other. That's NIMS and ICS in a nutshell— the whole history and story would be another book entirely, and you probably would not enjoy reading it. It is essential information and painfully dull to read and study. *Trust me.*

★★★★

Depending on the ICS structure, those given the decision-making authority will determine how steps are taken to address emergencies. Signification tasks, procedures, and delegations will be given out to prioritize activities such as allocating supplies, facilities, personnel, and resources.

★★★★

Emergency management is at its best when maintaining the ICS and ensuring all areas—command, operations, planning, logistics, intelligence and investigations, finance, and administration—are effectively facilitated and carried out. When decision-making authority is too widely dispersed, the incident managers' ability to identify critical concerns and delegate accordingly can be strictly limited. When this happens—often under urgent conditions—the response departments' quality of services can fail.

Decentralized Command Vs. Centralized Command

Whether made up of a handful of people or thousands of members, every organization will either have a centralized or a decentralized operational command structure.[17] Centralized command structures are top-down, where decisions, policies, and actions are decided at the highest leadership levels. There is a transparent chain of command in a centralized command structure. People are made aware of the information passed down directly from the source, usually the department's chief. A centralized command is often seen as the traditional company structure, where ultimately, *one person* is calling the shots. Centralized commands typically do not work well for large emergency events or large agencies. There is such an abundance of factors, responsibilities, and elements to make sure it goes smoothly. However, this does not keep people from choosing this model because they do not want their messages to be diluted or misinterpreted. Still, we see how it can create disastrous results in emergency events and situations. Imagine every time a police officer in a small, rural town wanted to pull someone over for speeding, but they needed to call for approval from the city's mayor to do it. That traffic stop might not be the best use of time management or practical for either party! This is where a decentralized command structure may be the better alternative.

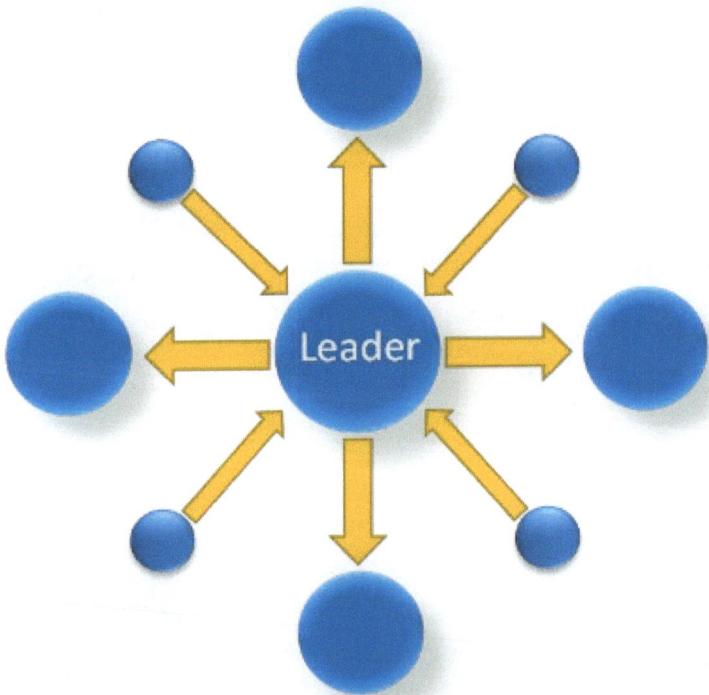

**Centralized
Command Structure
Model**

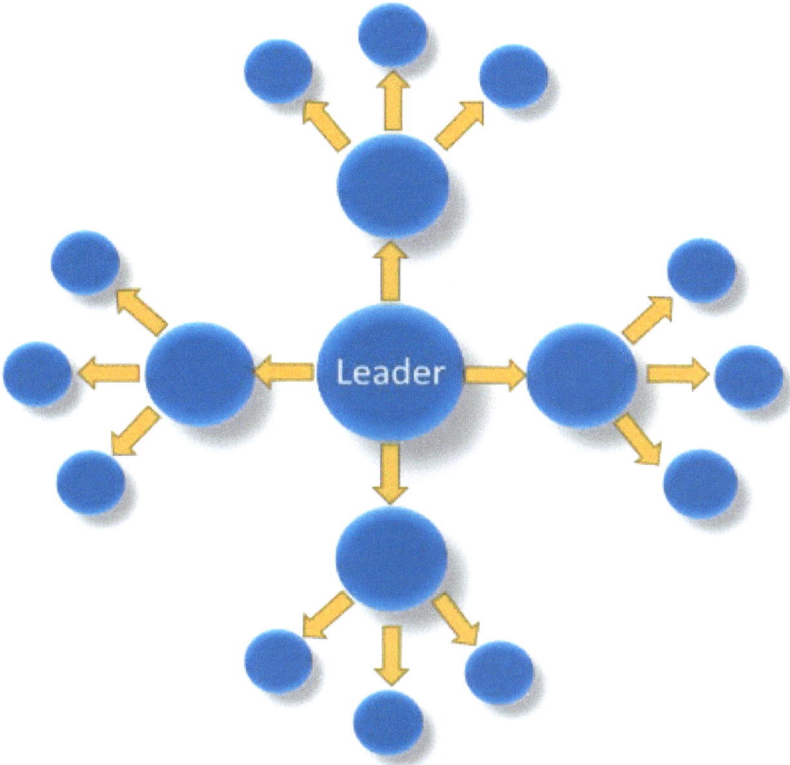

**Decentralized
Command Structure
Model**

Decentralized command structures or a combination of both types have gained popularity among private companies, especially within non-traditional organizations and start-ups in fields such as technology. A decentralized command allows problems to be solved at the *lowest possible level*, empowering first-line-management and multi-leveled staff to fulfill their duties while being entrusted to do them with their capabilities and skillsets. As more people are freed up to do what they were hired to do, so are the managers released to fulfill their roles and perform them to their greatest potential. Many organizations utilizing this structure, including emergency management teams, find that more of their employees stay longer, the processes move along quicker, and more significant goals are met and achieved.

So, what is the downfall? Well, have you ever played the telephone game, where you start by whispering a message in one person's ear, and by the time the message reaches the last person in the line, it is a totally different message altogether? Yes, that is the message dilution I was referring to. We can see how that can be problematic and the possibility of people receiving different orders from different people due to the disruption in communication in a decentralized structure.

★★★★

Federal vs. State vs. Local: What Are the Problems and the Roles of Each?

When a significant event happens, people will immediately ask, "Where is the federal government's response?" Take the most televised natural disaster in history, Hurricane Katrina, for example. Most citizens have huge misconceptions about the place and role of the federal government in emergencies and disasters, but more importantly, citizens do not understand the federal government's role *when* they intervene. They are unaware of how a federal response system works and its role and often forget about the enormous, neglected responsibilities the local and state municipalities and organizations have in their immediate area. **As I mentioned previously, one fundamental problem I have consistently found is agencies assume someone else is coming in to do the work.** That being said, it may be established as a standard operating procedure for departments under certain circumstances. One example is, in North Carolina, a sheriff may defer a murder investigation to the State Bureau of

Investigations (SBI) because they are more equipped to handle the investigation. Does that mean that the sheriff is now absolved of any responsibility for the incident? Absolutely not. The sheriff strengthens the working knowledge of his responding deputies in evidence preservation and securing the scene.

In an emergency or natural disaster, the local community—local emergency services, nonprofit organizations, for-profit [18] businesses, local governments, and volunteers—make up the first response agencies. There is a reason some of these individuals are called "first responders," for the locals will arrive first and know the lay of the land best. When there is a decentralized and bottom-up structure for local leaders to make rapid, efficient, and reliable decisions for relief efforts, it is a possible win-win for everyone affected by the disaster. The only issue is, if the event is beyond the budget and resources of the local government, the response may come to a stand-still until there is more money available. That is where the federal government's actual role begins: The President of the United States declares an emergency, and that frees up monies under the Stafford Act and unleashes the powerful wallet of the Federal Emergency Management Agency (FEMA). This has always been this way and will be for quite some time. The locals need to be prepared for executing the brunt of the work that has to be done, and they are the prime—sometimes, the only—choice to carry this out.

★★★★

When certain disasters are of such scale and magnitude that cities start to exhaust local and state resources, they ask the federal government to step in. However, in the event the federal government does become involved, this is usually more for funding reasons than response activities in the immediate timeframe. And when the federal government does step in, unfortunately, there is an excellent chance that their lack of promptness, risk-averse nature, and extra bureaucracy will prevent aid from effectively helping and reaching victims in a sufficient timeframe to mitigate the suffering from the immediate effects of the disaster.

For example, Hurricane Katrina[19] a category three storm during whose winds reached 120 miles per hour—hit Louisiana's coast on August 29th, 2005. And when the images of storm victims became breaking news, Americans across the country were appalled at the lack of response and assistance for those who were displaced and in need of food, water, and shelter. Many people, including an outspoken Kanye West, were critical of FEMA and President Bush [20] for waiting too long to respond.

★★★★

Among the Federal Government's Inherent Mistakes Were That:

- FEMA's executive suites were full of political appointees with little disaster experience.
- Millions of pounds of ice were delivered to holding centers in cities far away from the Gulf Coast, and FEMA ended up throwing out $100 million of unused ice.

- FEMA paid for 25,000 mobile homes, costing them $900 million, but since FEMA's regulations stated that such mobile homes could not be used on flood plains, many them could not be used.

- Hurricane Katrina's federal aid led to federal auditors estimating $1 billion or more in aid payments to individuals that were invalid.

- FEMA. turned away or blocked emergency supplies, volunteer doctors, private medical air transport for evacuations, water, and fuel supplies.

- There was "uncertainty over who was in charge" [21] and "incomprehensible red tape" preventing progress from happening.

The first bullet point is disturbingly true, and I know this firsthand. When I was asked to speak at the White House in 2014 for a round-table

discussion on innovation in emergency management programs, I met several appointed individuals who made a lasting impression on me.

I received great insight into why things *were* the way they were. The highest public office levels and their agencies had no previous experience or familiarity with handling emergencies, which spoke volumes about the state of affairs in FEMA and other federal agencies. One individual spoke candidly about taking basic courses under a false name and identity to avoid certain embarrassment in their position. This individual was an appointed member of the senior executive service of the federal government (SES). The SES is the civilian equivalent to generals in the military for federal agencies and is a position federal employees hope to achieve after decades of hard work and navigating the political "red tape" of the federal government. It is the highest they can go. And there I was, speaking to a person who was 20-something years old with no emergency management experience and a former presidential campaign manager for Barack Obama, holding this position for no other reason than President Obama won the election and rewarded them the position.

★★★★

Photo credit: Boston Globe (web;2020)

Hurricane Katrina initially shined the spotlight on the federal government's response issues and overtook the American public's television for months following. Years later, former President Obama said this of Katrina:

"What started out as a natural disaster became a man-made disaster—a failure of government to look out for its own citizens." [22]

Nonetheless, Kanye West and others were incorrect assuming that the federal government was responsible for the initial response since the local government was unprepared for a response under its governor and city mayor's leadership.

"If we were to rely on the federal government to be the primary responding agency, they would, no doubt, fail 100-percent of the time." — Craig Fugate, Secretary of FEMA

This statement is not because FEMA does not want to help people. They are just not structured to respond to every American city and town's emergencies, regardless of the event's scale, due to their complex emergency systems' nature. A much more viable and hope-filled route is to take the steps needed to build a robust local and state emergency response system, beginning with placing the emergency manager in its rightful place.

★★★★

Continuity of Government and Chain of Command

People and government alike need to know who is in charge when their most visible leadership—their mayor, governor, or local government agencies—is nowhere to be found during an event. The visibility and presence of emergency managers do need to increase. As an entrusted and relied-upon leader to both the public and its government, the emergency manager's rise is a critical step to progress, especially as we see all types of emergencies arising in society today. The emergency manager needs to be in place before an event happens, and this position should be made known to everyone. So, their authority is official— at the very least, on paper—to avoid confusion when disaster strikes again.

Before moving on to the next chapter, one other thing is that an essential aspect of moving every service under emergency management means that it can become scalable, regardless of which services may not be available. You can add or subtract services within emergency management. For example, adding a community-based arm of emergency management, or a new public safety entity, will maintain stability in the structure, activities, and first response.   Today, many are advocating for the defunding of the police. In this case, the emergency management will see that funding is shifted to enhance one of the other components to support the overall emergency response quality without losing this funding back into the city budget.

★★★★

CHAPTER 4

REDEFINING AUTHORITY

The question every department needs to ask, regardless of which city or town one is in, is "Who's available to fulfill emergency support services if the police are defunded?" With changes happening in recent months—mainly deciding to defund or disband police departments—communities and decision-makers need to figure out what will fill this missing void quickly.

With cities that don't have enough resources, there must be someone put in place to have the authority to uphold the law and ensure the public's safety. If you are removing power, you need to know who or what will replace it. If you do not, in some cases, the public will decide for you. And this usually only makes matters worse.

After I trained with the Center for Disease Control and Prevention, I became a certified designated infection control officer for my department. I found that this role had a tremendous amount of power to educate and make calls on behalf of the department and the public. For example, I was designated to decide when someone was or was not exposed to a bloodborne pathogen or some other form of infectious disease. It was challenging to explain to a person that was just vomited on that it probably won't count as an exposure. One thing I was taught was that "gross" does not always mean "exposed." Easier said than done, though.

These types of decisions included who needed to be out of work, what the incubation period would be, and when individuals were permitted to return to work. As an infection control officer, I was given a "statement-of-authority" to make these decisions on behalf of the department's chief as the subject matter expert. I still marvel at the level of power and responsibility this gave me on the public's behalf.

★★★★

As an emergency manager, your authority does need to be defined. It is crucial to have a statement-of-authority granted to you to take the lead in certain circumstances, especially, for example, in a sheltering situation. With a statement-of-authority, you become the mini-mayor or the subject matter expert, giving you the ability to make choices for the sake of keeping the public healthy and informed. However, I found that people are often not aware of the statement-of-authority. Most individuals don't even know this document exists today.

★★★★

Statements-of-Authority

Obtaining statements-of-authority is your first step as an emergency manager. Without them, you cannot do your job. With it, you will be empowered to do a specific task and make the crucial decisions that need to be made to help move through emergencies and disasters as smoothly as possible. Just as police officers are given the authority to make arrests, you will also need to officially be given the power to lead and take emergency matters into your own hands.

The process is quite simple. The head of the department usually requests a statement-of-authority for the individual to be granted from the elected powers-that-be. The statement-of-authority is approved and vested by the elected leadership of the assigned municipality. With each statement-of-authority having its limitations, it still typically covers a wide span of topics and extensive areas in managing emergencies. The statement-of-authority will usually bring in monetary sources, as well. Funds can be used for various things— including food, water, sandbags, or first-aid kits, in some cases. This authority is significant in carrying out the emergency management tasks that need to get done. Having these funds will allow you to skip the many steps it usually takes to purchase items. You don't want to be asking for money during an incident that needs to be appropriated, voted on, or held up by political red tape. So, regardless of the town or city you represent, be sure to get your statement-of-authority.

★★★★

Here are additional steps any new emergency manager can use when undertaking a new emergency manager position:

1. Gain the official authority required to do your job. Be appointed, elected, or receive the statement-of-authority to allow you to operate freely and accordingly.
2. Review and audit existing plans, no matter how old they are. Do your best not to reinvent the wheel. Use what works and fix what doesn't.
3. Find existing "Single Points of Failure" and fix them immediately.
4. Find out your immediate capabilities and resources available in your area of operations.
5. Test your immediate capabilities as they stand.
6. Do not assume anything will "just happen."
7. Understand what support agreements and mutual aid agreements already exist or need to be established and their importance to your overall success.

8. Get to know your community on a personal level and listen to their concerns for emergency preparedness. This is an excellent method to use if you are overwhelmed at the beginning of your planning process and establish a reliable, informed starting point.

9. Speak with all departments about a single issue to see where planning and communication have failed in the past.

10. Speak with neighboring cities or counties to understand outside capabilities and assets and feel for their existing relationship. If there is bad blood or hesitation, work to resolve it as quickly as possible.

11. Establish your budget, and be prepared to explain how you will attain program longevity and sustainability year over year.

12. Develop a community-based program, such as a CERT, so you have trained, vetted, and identifiable volunteers. FEMA already establishes this program, and all training materials are free and available online with the curriculum.

★★★★

Elected or Appointed?

In the city you serve, you'll need to talk to city leadership and figure out how emergency managers are given their roles and responsibilities, whether by a statement-of-authority, by vote, or by appointment. I sometimes come across it when the statement-of-authority is avoided, and people are appointed to emergency leadership roles, such as the example with FEMA. But 99-percent of the time, emergency managers are neither elected nor appointed. Sadly, leadership can grant the title of an emergency manager to someone who, as an example, was on light duty because of a broken wrist and then needs to be given a temporary role. Sometimes, specific individuals are hired, voted in, or appointed because they are a "close friend" or the elected leadership's acquaintance. A 'figurehead' appointment typically does not pan out well since these people come into their roles with very little applicable knowledge and experience in the field. When real emergencies arise, they have very little to contribute.

An example of an elected operational position is the position of a county sheriff. A sheriff is elected to their office and is not required to have any law enforcement experience. They are a representative of their community for law enforcement and prison matters. I agree with this since I view the sheriff's role, regardless of it being a political appointment, as being in the community's best interest for a specific task. Sheriffs that I have worked with have always put the right people in to support their offices.

Another example of an elected position is the county register of deeds. Even though the appointment is a four-year term, no one seems to know what this person is responsible for, and nobody bothers to question this. Somewhat similar to the emergency manager's role.

★★★★

With most cities pulling in personnel to make up an emergency management team or having an individual designated as the coordinator of emergency management on top of their regular duties, the only city I know of that hired a dedicated emergency manager with authority was Detroit.

In this case, Kevyn Orr, a former bankruptcy lawyer, was hired to help pull the city out of financial ruin and prevent an economic collapse. Still, he was bestowed an emergency manager's title to fill a particular need the city of Detroit was facing. Today, the emergency manager can look significantly different, depending on what situations and issues towns are currently facing. My hope is for greater consistency in this role and local governments' organizational structure, so there is a better chance of systemic processes of getting things done, especially during disasters. [23]

★★★★

In many cities and various federal government agencies, I noticed that those who were under the emergency management umbrella were usually an officer or an employee fulfilling an additional role due to injury or—for lack of a better term—punishment (a.k.a. "desk duty"). It was a clear reflection of management not knowing or understanding what emergency management was. Therefore, there was no actual, appointed emergency manager to properly orchestrate all the communities' projects, disasters, and needs. Instead of having an emergency management department, what often is created is a "catch-all" or "place holder" group that may be formed as a collateral duty to a fire or police department. Because of a lack of training and emergency management experience, these groups often overlooked one vital aspect: creating and training Community Emergency Response Team (CERT) members. Whether a part of a fire or police department or not, these volunteers will hold meetings, fulfill emergency manager functions, and prepare for a response—such as a large event— while the department chief typically remains the authority. These individuals are volunteers assigned to provide emergency services for the public, albeit limited during emergency events for their safety.

Some cities will choose to train local church members so that these CERT members will be activated in large-scale disasters like earthquakes, floods, and hurricanes. When I've led emergency management, I would need to muster CERT groups, ask each person to show their CERT identification to show that they were trained, and delegate tasks among them. CERT volunteers would also be given radios, vests, helmets, gear, and directions for whatever project they were assigned to. One CERT volunteer would shut off power or water to affected homes. Another would be asked to set up a first-aid station. Another would potentially do light search and rescue or administrative duties, etc. These examples are why I am a massive proponent of CERT in your community. CERT training and teams provide wide-spread community cohesion and support.

CERT is quite the opposite of make-shift social justice movements, where the community members, such as those involved with the Capitol Hill Autonomous Zone (CHAZ), insist they'll 'figure out' what they'll do on their own in case of emergencies and restrict the police force's presence. But again, this type of behavior and ignorance typically only endangers those in their communities since the lack of preparedness, equipment, and training can lead to a lack of emergency support and help.

★★★★

Emergency Manager as A Liaison in the Community

One of the leading roles each emergency manager fills is to liaise with the community and working groups. You can think of this role as similar to social services. Often, the department chiefs will not want to engage in this role with the community, feeling like it's not up to them to take care of it or personally not want to do the job. The emergency manager will need to take this responsibility by going face-to-face with the public, identifying what the unique needs are in the community precisely, and leading appropriate community-based services.

One type of task force I took part in was a hoarding task force. This service was mainly for older adults or intellectually handicapped persons who won't leave their house and start hoarding trash, newspapers, boxes, or objects they *mentally* cannot dispose of properly. This habit creates enormous fire hazards and health hazards in their homes. So, a task force was delegated to mitigate this issue by going into the houses in conjunction with social services, bringing in a dumpster, arranging sanitation, and clearing out the excess stored in homes. Often, when we activated these task forces, many people would appreciate and tell us they didn't have money or means to handle all the items they've accumulated over the years. Making this kind of direct impact helps solve problems in the community and help people stay safer.

Another task force operated was an elder abuse task force related to ensuring the elderly community was not facing neglect from their families and could stay healthy during extreme weather conditions. Since many older adults didn't have air conditioning or their public housing HVAC units failed in the summer, they often became dehydrated, putting them at risk for injury and even death. Those people serving on this task force noticed that many elderly individuals hadn't spoken to their families or children in years. They were then left to fend for themselves, and we usually found they could not solve their problems very quickly. To resolve this for them, we brainstormed how we could set up shelters and ways we could give them access to places with bathrooms, water, and air conditioning. The elderly could stay there during the daytime in the summer while the temperatures were at their highest and then go home at night when temperatures had cooled down. With services like these, as the emergency manager, I was the face of it all. I would show up, and people knew who I was and that I was there to help. It was a gratifying feeling. This presence allowed us to build rapport with the community members by giving them a chance to know us.

Another example of a community-based task force is nuisance properties or vacant and abandoned homes. In North Carolina, there houses that either someone neglected or abandoned, such as dilapidated farmhouses. But to think this is only a rural occurrence is mistaken. In metro Boston, we also had abandoned buildings from large companies or old government buildings that placed fences around them and left them. The police weren't going to go in there, and sometimes, these buildings find use as shelters for drug use and other criminal activities, such as prostitution. One year, during a heavy snowstorm, two of the buildings where people were going in and out collapsed due to the snow's weight. The department sent out a task force, in waist-high snow, to go in and pull the rubble out with cadaver dogs as a rescue-and-recovery effort. The emergency manager's decision to start different task forces depends on the issues prominent in your community.

★★★★

Regardless of where you operate as an emergency manager, it would be best to be involved in the community and keep your eyes open to see what is happening in the jurisdiction. There are good reasons for groups such as the above-listed task forces—if there is a need for them. Emergency managers develop and start committees for any community issues that need the resolution to aid in the citizens' welfare, especially since the chiefs of departments may not have time to address these issues over other pressing public safety matters. The possibilities and social problems are endless regarding what type of committees and task forces should be created.

With CHAZ, both the private and public resources in the community were affected. The opportunity presented itself for an emergency manager to liaise with community leaders and business owners to introduce mitigation techniques to resolve the issues. This would require a more extensive role since racial divide and law enforcement reception compound this scenario. The emergency manager here would play an integral function of the mediator, who would also need to be a liaison to the police, fire department, and public works to keep the peace while solving current issues and cleaning up the area. They would have to absorb the brunt of the angry community and address their problems, as well.

★★★★

Identification of What Your Community Needs

As the emergency manager, when you start to identify your community needs, don't be naive in thinking only certain things happen in particular communities—i.e., dilapidated buildings. Regardless of the prominent issues, stay open-minded, objective, and accept what needs to be addressed. Keep in mind some widespread problems, such as the opioid epidemic. No city is exempt from drugs and drug overdoses: what varies is just the cultural differences. It is an issue when autonomous groups such as CHAZ or Antifa form, and citizens are not sure what the next steps are to combat them. My concern in these cases is that they blindly reject emergency responses, and law enforcement hasn't been welcomed into these communities. The big issue here is that the leaders and those in the community have no idea how to offer medical and hygiene services, emergency services, or specific services. There are significant concerns when these self-appointed groups do not have any leadership or answers. This, from what

I've seen, is not safe or sustainable. What if the city cuts off the water or electricity? What if there's a hurricane inbound? How will we respond if there's another injury or shooting? When preparedness for events and activities is ill-prepared, these questions cannot be answered. But the emergency manager's role in situations like this has to have the solutions to all of these questions and plan accordingly.

★★★★

Second Amendment Armed Protests and Reduction of Police Security

I have recently seen new ways groups gather and protest while armed with rifles and various firearms. This situation happened recently at Stone Mountain Park, near Atlanta, Georgia, where a predominantly black militant group protested the monument representing white supremacy. These 200-armed men and women were legally carrying rifles, under the second amendment right to bear arms, and were marching in formation to protest. Why do I have to mention race? Unfortunately, because we have to account for the root of the protest and the reality of the situation to prepare for the possibility that others may choose to retaliate solely based on a skin color different from their own. It is ugly and unfair, but as an emergency manager, I have to look at the totality of the circumstances, form a realistic judgment of what could happen, and figure out the possible ways to safeguard the community. You cannot choose the situation; however, you must act when it presents itself.

★★★★

There's now a paradigm shift and dynamic change to how people are protesting. Social media's weaponization provides a platform for 'riots on-demand' and overwhelming situations that exceed a community's available resources for an immediate response. Who will handle an armed situation if the police are defunded or disbanded? That question is a prime example of dealing with the reality of the situation. I've personally never dealt with a problem involving a city or municipality defunding the police department. It is a new situation an emergency manager will face moving forward with little to no guidance. Who will manage it? The emergency manager, utilizing foresight, emergency preparedness, would include being hospital ready, putting together trauma kits for CERT, and training people to treat gunshots and burn wounds within the community should an armed opposition take place. With Antifa groups pelting officers with commercial-grade fireworks, metal fire extinguishers, and others lighting people on fire with kerosene, how will emergency management respond?

Groups, especially those in large numbers, feel empowered and bold because there are often no repercussions for their actions, and they know there's a good chance they will get away with what wrong they are doing. And now, the police are limited in how they can arrest citizens and enforce the law. They don't have the available manpower to stop crowds, and at times, they can feel helpless just standing there with hands tied due to bureaucratic public appeasement. Not only do mayors of towns and cities need to know what they will do if their departments suffer a reduction, but emerging emergency managers also have to be forward-thinking since many movements like these are on entirely new ground and spreading rapidly.

★★★★

CHAPTER 5

STRATEGIC PLANNING

Understanding the Importance of Process.

For a specialty area like emergency management, people often underestimate or overlook the importance of examining the process. When you focus on the process, you gain a greater understanding of how things work. You also gain greater insight into planning, spotting errors and omissions, and relying on a specific operating model that guides you and produces uniformity in your work—this technique aids in creating complete plans. The understanding of the process is exceptionally vital for being prepared for any disaster or event. Emergency managers need to know how to quickly fix what issues appear at a moment's notice and have the wherewithal to know what initiatives will fail and knowledge to correct them immediately.

Many of the plans I review or audit seem complete to leadership and the individuals that produce them. But issues arise when you put the plan into action. Looking at the process, here's an example to help you relate and understand this in emergency management planning.

If you ask an individual to write a plan for changing a flat tire on a car from start to finish, they will probably get it about 75% right, even if they are an automotive mechanic. But if you ask them to dig a bit further and state that they feel comfortable that their plan is complete – would they feel confident giving it to a person that had never driven a car before or changed a flat tire?

You will find their thought process to have doubt and issues beginning to surface. The devil is in the details. If I ask them if their initial first step is still the *same as* the first step in their initial written plan? It usually becomes the third or fourth step in their complete plan. Walk it through your mind and visualize the actual process for a minute and see if you can do it. I'll put the questions I would ask on the following page, so you don't cheat.

The above example is similar to how most plans appear when I am conducting an audit. On paper, having all of the essential elements listed makes leadership happy. In many cases, this would stand alone as complete because questions have answers. And leadership often becomes comfortable and confident with knowing they have the minimum they require—on paper, that is.

★★★★

Additional Questions for changing your tire:

Did you think to write
1. "Make sure the car is off?"
2. "Set the emergency brake?"
3. "Open the trunk."
4. "Check to see if you have a spare tire?"
5. "Find the tire iron."

If you did – you are already using the process in your favor!

★★★★

Accepting and Understanding the Reality of the Situation

One way to look at a problem that seems impossible to solve is to know a solution exists. In other words, can you do what you need to do, or is it impossible? Is there an obstacle or two standing in your way of achieving the goals you've set? An acceptable representation of this is a model ship in a bottle. At first, it seems impossible to get a ship through the opening, but the fact remains that somehow, someway, it got in there in the first place – even if you don't immediately know how it happened.

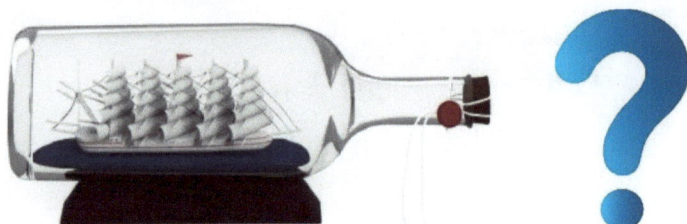

Try looking at the problem in reverse order. Doing this can help you see exactly how your process is working, creating issues, or placing a speed bump in front of you. If there is a tangible result and you just don't know how yet -- it is achievable just like a ship in a bottle.

★★★★

For example, if you want to plan a route to a hospital, you may ask ten different people and get ten similar answers. But look at your end objective of getting to the hospital in reverse. You can see that all of the different opinions arrive at the same conclusion – getting to the hospital (the goal) is achievable.

Now, if you work backward from the goal, you can begin to eliminate some of the directions that do not work in your plan's best interest. Instead of trying all of the routes out and wasting valuable time on the ones that don't meet your goal efficiently, you may know from experience that some of the roads have low bridges and apparatus cannot fit under them, or maybe one route works best at 7:00 am but not at 4:00 pm due to rush hour traffic. It is always possible **the most direct route is not the fastest route** due to stoplights and traffic. Try getting past Fenway Park on a Saturday afternoon in the summer when the Red Sox have a home game! You will need to know the best routes to and from Boston hospitals for all times of the day and night.

We are examining how having the right knowledge and experience will change your entire thought process and approach in this example. My point being, you can't just list "go to the hospital" in a plan and expect to get there when needed, if at all. By working in reverse from the goal to the individual elements required to complete that goal, you will have saved energy, time, and valuable resources in your planning processes through elimination. You always have to look beyond the goal and understand the process, and working in reverse helps trim the fat of your time management wasted going down the wrong path. You may form a few different plans based on what you find, and that is a good thing!

★★★★

Pre-planning

Many leaders, including emergency managers, make a common mistake when misconceptions affect the pre-planning process. While many individuals would like to take a straightforward approach to strategy and assume things will happen a certain way, such as other municipalities' assets and equipment will be readily available to borrow—these are actual single-points-of-failure when the time comes to depend on them.

It is essential to do some legwork, know precisely what you're asking for, and have tried-out, practiced, and tested theories, methods, and approaches beforehand. Again, don't just write it onto paper and hope that it happens. Ask, "Does what I'm planning to do work in reality?" This sounds basic, but many leaders feel prepared enough with ideas and equipment but have not held exercises and carried out the process to see if it will work. Even though some of this may feel like a trial-and-error process, it is safer and wiser to do this now in the planning process than during a real emergency or disaster, where people's lives, property, and the environment are at stake.

Here's a similar scenario expanding on the last one involving getting to the hospital. If victims need to be rushed to a hospital during a mass-casualty event, what does your process look like? Some leaders will decide to 'go to the closest hospital.' The issue that often arises with this decision is having no regard for traffic patterns, especially during rush hours. Traffic, especially in metropolitan cities, can be a significant deterrent in reaching hospitals in time. And this can delay the healthcare of victims, and at times, puts their lives in jeopardy. A hospital ten miles out may be closed when its route is clear of traffic. Another question overlooked is how many patients each hospital can hold; is it an appropriate level of care hospital, like a level one trauma center, or is it a community-based hospital specializing in stitches and flu shots? When leaders and decision-makers are not thinking about specific things, plans can be riddled with issues. At times, they forget that outside-the-box thinking and solutions can be more effective in reality. **Again, in emergency management, the most direct route may not be the *fastest* route.**

Planning

When most people write a plan, they write a simple "point A to point B plan" from start to finish. Since most planning steps can be static and linear, things are not expected to change suddenly. No adaptations need to be made; in other words, no "additional plan B or C or D." In emergency management, this plan *must* be flexible. The overall effectiveness of emergency management plans is best when they are dynamic, holistic, and malleable. Some aspects of planning are

RISE OF THE EMERGENCY MANAGER

in your control; most things will not be due to the fluid circumstances. I will talk about that in "Left of Bang" planning in the chapter.

Plan "A" vs. Plan "B"

Most emergency managers and planners that are new to the position work hard on their plan A. It is usually a bit over-complicated and filled with ideas that may or may not work, depending on what the topic is they are covering. The fact that there is a plan in place at all is quite an accomplishment. However, you cannot rest on your laurels. Once you feel that your plan is complete, it is essential always to go back and make it better. But what does that mean? It means that you need to make an additional plan that can back up your original if things go wrong.

For example, let's say you are planning to fix your car. You work out a budget, order your parts, and once they arrive, you get to work. Then, you accidentally snap a bolt or cut a broken line. What now? You call the mechanic as quickly as possible and arrange a tow truck to get the problem solved. Plan "B" usually costs a bit of money to achieve the same result, but it also typically relieves you of time, stress, and wasted effort.

★★★★

An excellent example on the emergency management side would be concerning temporary sheltering. For instance, if a public nursing home lost heat in the winter, would it be more beneficial to open a temporary shelter to care for the elderly until their HVAC units were repaired? Or is it more helpful to have a support agreement with a local hotel to provide vouchers for the senior citizens to stay there? There is no right or wrong answer, but you can see the benefits of both concerning time, money, effort, and budget—a simple plan "A" and plan "B."

The Plan Itself

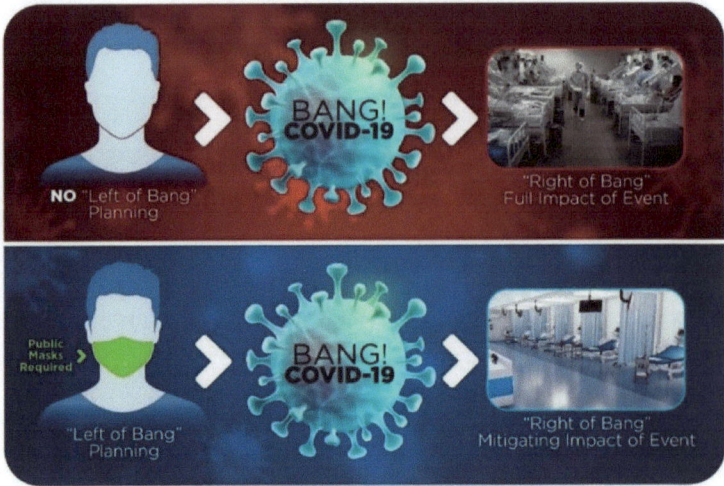

There are typically (3) three *phases* to the outline of an emergency management plan, each requiring different levels of individual plans:

1. **PHASE I:** *"Left of Bang"*
2. **PHASE II:** *"The Bang"*
3. **PHASE III:** *"Right of Bang"*

★★★★

"Left of Bang"

PHASE I: *Pre-planning*

The Only Time When Things Are In Your Total Control.

Before COVID-19 hit in early 2020, most public infection control programs relied on existing methods and vaccinations to help prevent the spread of diseases. The world never thought there would be a new disease capable of decimating the population with no way to stop it. If we take the world's preparations before the disease struck, we will look at this as "left of bang planning," or pre-planning, for the event. This section of the planning will ultimately lessen the impact of an event if done correctly.

★★★★

"The Bang"

PHASE II:

The Event Happens. Your Plan Will Now Be Put To The Test.

"The Bang" is part two of emergency management planning. Bang represents what happens when the event hits, whether expected or unexpected. Usually, the event occurs and expands so rapidly that the only thing that can slow it down is what you have included in your "Left of Bang" pre-planning. If nothing was done to pre-plan, then you can expect the full impact of the event.

★★★★

"Right of Bang"
PHASE III

The Event is Prolonged or Concluding

What did you forget to plan for or not expect? Did your preplanning work or need improvement? What were the issues that you missed in the planning process? Right of Bang is the planning that is done focusing on *after* the event has happened. It is incredibly unpredictable, but you can mitigate that with some forward-thinking. The most important aspect of "Right of Bang" is what you learned for the next time and how you will apply it to your revised "Left of Bang" pre-planning for future events.

★★★★

Here are some tips and recommendations for you as you create the three parts of emergency management planning:

As emergency managers, what are you doing to prepare for the hurricane, tornado, earthquake, shooting, or any disaster that is impending?

A.   **Keep making your "Left of Bang" better!** Refine it, add to it, and continuously improve this part, since you have the time to do it now. It is an **on-going cycle with no end**.

B.   **"The Bang" phase has commenced.** Once the event happens, the **"Left of Bang" is behind you.** In this stage, you will see how things are executed, and the actual operational part of the plan takes action. This is not the time to focus on your mistakes—make a note and move on to correct the things you can while driving things **forward**.

C. **"Right of Bang"** After the event is over, then comes recovery! The main questions are:

1. Did your plans work, and what did you learn?
2. Did your plan help bring everything back to the way things were?
3. What else needs to be created or implemented
4. for future events?
5. If your planning worked, what can you do to make your planning work better?
6. In what *other* situations can you apply these same lessons?

★★★★

While some aspects of planning during Left of Bang remain static—like things, places, vehicles, equipment that are always there, etc.—it is vital to secure these things and have them ready to go.

Then, dynamic elements relate to the "Bang" and "Right of Bang" phases. Sometimes, things become totally out of your control. For this reason, you will need to be flexible in the application of these plans. You are dealing with things as they happen to you in *real-time,* and outcomes may be predictable or completely unpredictable. Remember to expect that items become fluid and continuously moving, so it's best to be ready since you never know exactly what will happen in these phases.

Like the Boxing Champ, Mike Tyson spoke concerning his preparation for a title fight, *"Everyone has a plan until you get punched in the face."*
Prepare to be punched in the face.

The Single Point of Failure

One of the most critical aspects of your planning will be avoiding a catastrophic failure on your part, known as "the single point of failure." I mentioned this term a few paragraphs ago regarding assumptions of other municipalities' equipment. The single point of failure is when your plan has no redundancy or back-up. As the name implies, the single point of failure places too much emphasis on one aspect of your planning working correctly; in other words, you assume something so simple could not derail your entire plan. But it will, and when it does, there will be no one to blame but yourself.

Single points of failure can be anything in your plan that can force the entirety of your execution to come to a screeching halt. Some examples are your only available vehicle breaking down or using a single vendor for a specific supply item, only to find they went out of business a year prior—and you never updated your plans. Single points of failure come in many forms, and you need to be aware of their existence in your planning process. They are easy to avoid but also easy to miss. Eliminating all single points of failure will not only aid in your planning and execution going smoothly but also lend credibility to your level of professionalism as a thorough and experienced emergency management planner.

★★★★

The Support Agreement

In emergency management planning, support agreements are the backbone of your plans. They are the pre-established service agreements with private entities, private sector assets, pre-contracts, resources, and businesses. They are a significant way to get millions of dollars of services made available to you for a fraction of the cost.

Support Agreements include:

- **A description of available services and products.**
- **Established and agreed upon pricing.**
- **Limitations and scalability.**
- **The duration of the services.**
- **A retainer for immediate priority and delivery of services during set events.**
- **Allowable miscellaneous reimbursements and by-line pricing items.**

In a recent example, a support agreement alleviated the 2020 toilet paper shortage during the coronavirus pandemic. The supply of toilet paper became non-existent in many stores, one group whose toilet paper inventory stayed the same during this time: the major hotel chains. Hotel chains continued to receive continuous delivery of toilet paper because hotels are pre-contracted with vendors. Vendors have a legal obligation to provide toilet paper to the hotel because of a prearranged agreement. So, if vendors do not deliver, it would be a breach of contract. This would allow hotels to have the legal right to sue these suppliers, regardless of the circumstances *not* listed in the agreement. Supermarkets like your local Target and Costco, being distributors, do not have these contracts in place, causing an absence of toilet paper for many consumers across the country without recourse to the suppliers. Therefore, it is vital to have support agreements in place before any disaster occurs.

When I was the Director for Pinkerton's Washington D.C., Maryland, Delaware, and Pennsylvania field offices, I learned that Pinkerton—which operates in 100 countries as a trusted risk advisor to over 90-percent of the Fortune 1000 companies— has a similar thing when a support agreement is in place.

★★★★

The following paragraph is a real-life example to explain the benefits of a strong support agreement. A CEO who has traveled to Mexico called me and said, "they need an armored car, three armed guards, an interpreter, and a GPS tracking device in case of kidnapping." I provide this service at a moment's notice without hesitation. I say, "Here's the price, and it'll be ready in one hour." The price even included the VAT tax or the "foreign tax on US services" How is this possible, you may ask? I think you know what the answer is.

This is an example of having an up-to-date support agreement contract in place. It contained all of the agreed-upon services and rates, so both parties know what to expect in-advance; there was no debate or argument. An agreement like this can make all the difference when you're in a crisis and need things to move quickly. By saving hours negotiating prices, service items, availability, and delivery timeframes, pre-existing support agreements are critical to successful emergency response. **These are legal documents** that both party's attorneys read through and approved far in advance of any service request.

★★★★

I've said it before -- locality doesn't matter. In rural North Carolina, you may know who owns a tractor, a boat, a tow truck—all things we might urgently need one day. To set up a support agreement, you could, for example, contact Mr. Smith, who has a snowplow, and ask Mr. Smith if we have a snowstorm what he would charge for an hour's worth of snow plowing. I might ask how many other people he could provide to help with this? And then, Mr. Smith would share the cost and subtle details he would require to perform the service. Once we agree on these details, I would send Mr. Smith a binding written contract for the next year and a deposit of, say, $1,000. If the services are not needed that year, the $1,000 will be kept by Mr. Smith as a retainer until the contract is revisited the following year. This allows us to renegotiate as needed without a coverage gap—like if gas prices rise or minimum wage is higher, at least everything is now in place to move forward if his services are needed immediately. The other alternative is to buy a snowplow for $3,000 that I may never use and have to store and maintain.

Emergency managers with limited funding available must utilize private resources often. The key to arranging a million dollars' worth of services with a fraction of the available money is to get a support agreement binding with a retainer. A retainer secures the support agreement between the two parties for the specific services contracted upfront. This technique is successful because you will not require all of the different services in your support agreements simultaneously. There is no way for emergency managers to buy all the equipment and services they need when an emergency arises quickly, both due to time constraints and money. It is a matter of maximizing the resources available to you by taking the time to secure these support agreements where you are shorthanded or not capable of delivering during a crisis.

★★★★

In foresight, whatever you anticipate would be needed is what you will proactively need to pursue. This way, whether for a flood, a parade, or a shooting, we'd know whether to go to public works, the local country club or to food services and create a contract beforehand. Through collaboration and partnerships, major and minor problems and anticipated disasters can be mitigated or solved through a small budget used appropriately – **"Don't use a $100 solution to a $1 problem."** Learn how to stretch a dollar.

★★★★

Mutual Aid Agreements

On the public side, mutual aid agreements are public sector assets, reciprocal, and work in tandem between you and the group you're working with. They are between neighboring agencies and used to boost available manpower or equipment coverage for events. These are called mutual aid agreements because both parties agree to provide the services to each other as needed, rather than paying for the services each time they are used.

Some counties will have the equipment you don't have, or they'll be willing to help out in your area. As a result, both parties will benefit while receiving equal value with a doubled workforce and additional available equipment. Through mutual aid agreements, outside specialists can be gained, and the scope of the positive impact made expands for everybody. I have found that with mutual aid agreements, nine out of ten times, it becomes a win-win for everyone involved.

★★★★

There are some significant issues with relying solely on mutual aid that you should be aware of:

1. Coverage may not always be available within the resources if they are already being used or deployed.
2. The exchange of services may not be of equal value or type of service.
3. Because the equipment is used often during regular duties, it may not be available due to breakdowns, accidents, or lack of neighboring manpower to deliver and operate the equipment when budgets are cut.
4. If one community becomes reliant on another community resource without reciprocating, the agreement can be terminated.

★★★★

It is generally wise not to become dependent on a specific party's services or equipment. I give this warning because it is not uncommon for access to valuable resources, and the next day, the other party is prioritizing their services and cannot help you at that time. What will you do in these instances?

My recommendation here is to have multiple counties as partners, especially those outside of your immediate area. This helps and encourages everyone to collaborate and obtain successful working relationships. You may realize that you need things you didn't plan for. In this case, it is always appreciated when you take a moment to say a "professional thank you" for sending equipment or extra personnel in your time of need. And by "professional thank you," I mean pizzas.

This can help you plan better and plan for the next year while communicating to the other party to budget for this new item. In the long run, it helps both parties and saves you a lot of money by not spending funds to obtain whatever you need.

★ ★ ★ ★

Grants

Another great way to do more with less is through grants. It makes sense to see what kind of grants are available for what you need since there are grants for almost everything today. Unfortunately, too many people—including emergency managers—don't look at grants, which can supply you with items on your wish list. Nowadays, everything in emergency services is available through all types of grants. Whether it is equipment, vehicles, supplies, or a program you want to get up and run, it is worth investing your time in researching and applying for grants, even if it's only for $5,000 or $500,000. Grants are out there for you and are available for those who'll put the time and energy in to apply for them. They are available through private, state, and federal programs; so, don't limit yourself to one type or method.

★★★★

Leasing vs. Purchasing

With a limited budget and the same idea of mutual aid agreements, it is much savvier to lease than to buy. For example, if I need a new pick-up truck to transport my equipment, while many cities will budget money to buy one, I recommend emergency managers lease one instead. Let's say it costs $60,000 to buy a new pick-up truck, but with leasing, one saves so much money per year. When you lease, you can free up a large percentage of funds. Even saving up to $20,000 each year will allow you to purchase or lease other things you need. One simple example: while I was at Pinkerton, we were scheduled to do a movie premiere, a museum opening, and the Oscars with dignitaries and A-List celebrities attending. Instead of spending thousands of dollars on new radios, needing to program and update them beforehand, and hope they all worked, we had a support agreement set up with a local security vendor. This vendor asked me how many radios I needed, and we received them for the duration of the event based on our support agreement. Did we suddenly need more radios? Did we need additional earpieces for the personal protection detail? Did any of the radios not work correctly? How about spare radios? We had to contact the vendor, and it would not be our issue but theirs. Leasing allows emergency managers to save time, money, and energy while also giving them peace of mind in many scenarios.

In summary, understanding the process in emergency management is essential to smart responses and success. Keeping in mind the Left of Bang, Bang, and Right of Bang planning phases, emergency managers should be as prepared as possible and be flexible as unexpected events happen. Support agreements, mutual aid agreements, grants, and leasing are also indispensable and keyways for emergency management responses to be ready, take appropriate action steps and help everything return to its norm as smoothly and quickly as possible.

★★★★

CHAPTER 6

PROXYISM: DEFINING THE NEW AGE OF TERRORISM

With the recent peak in terrorist activity worldwide, this has also been the case within the U.S., with far-right terror acts leading the way. [25] Domestic terrorism has multiplied and has become just as much of a threat as foreign terrorism. In contrast to the types of terrorism the U.S. has dealt with in the past, extreme political polarization [26] and online communication power like social media have created new routes for homegrown terrorism to be constructed. Since 9/11, the diversity of domestic terrorism and its ideologies has increased. "From al-Qaeda and the Islamic

State to ethnically motivated [27] and anti-authority violent extremism, dangers on the digital landscape, and more sophisticated and easily available weapons, such as drones" have been on the rise in the past several years. Domestic terrorism[28] is generally defined as when a domestic terrorist is involved in terrorist activities on the homeland. These activities include any criminal and dangerous acts threatening human life, even if there's merely an intention to intimidate, influence, or affect the homeland's citizens or the homeland's government.

★★★★

The *New Age of Terrorism* became prominent with the Black Lives Matter movement, but to even state this is not that simple. While we give the Black Lives Matter movement the benefit of the doubt, the fact remains that every time they call for a peaceful protest or rally, Antifa follows suit with destruction and chaos. Antifa or other anti-fascist groups, including an estimated 200 groups in the U.S. as of August 2017— have claimed responsibility for many domestic incidents involving violence to advance their agenda. [29] While Black Lives Matter does not claim any responsibility for Antifa's actions, they maintain that their protests are peaceful demonstrations. This act is supported by the constitution and legal, as long as there is a permit granted. But anytime a Black Lives Matter protest happens, rioting, arson, violence, and murder are often part of the result. This happens through Proxyism— when a separate group causes unlawful mayhem on behalf of the host group, while the host group assures, they are only professing a peaceful message.

Recently, there have been protests every day in Washington, D.C. When I worked adjacent to the White House, I always gave myself extra time to drive due to the people who block off streets and cause additional traffic. If you look closely, you will see that Antifa tends to only show up for Black Lives Matter rallies, perhaps because they know the Black Lives Matter events guarantee TV and media coverage. Now and again, someone from Black Lives Matter acknowledges these steps by Antifa. Simultaneously, no one from Black Lives Matter will tell anyone at Antifa to stop their activities, denounce their association with their movement, or communicate to Antifa that they are clouding the message they are putting forth into society. So, this phenomenon, where the two go hand-in-hand, continues.

★★★★

Proxyism is a term I developed to describe clandestine terrorism or terrorism through a second party or proxy. Illegal acts can occur towards groups or on an individual's behalf to coerce governments while under the guise of a more significant movement. With the Black Lives Matter movement combined with Antifa activity, we see a virtual yin-yang or good-attached-to-evil framework.

In this situation, the two groups have a form of symbiosis that allows them to utilize each other. Both groups advance their objectives like hurricanes gaining power as they rip across the land with this relationship. This phenomenon is why Proxyism is so alarming. Domestic terrorism disguised as a noble cause is what I consider the *new age* of terrorism. I believe this relationship needs to have a term to describe the dynamic, so we can establish what encompasses it and separates it from, for lack of a better term, "classic" terrorism. That term is:

PARASITIC SYMBIOSIS

While there is no universal definition for terrorism today, one generally used description of terrorism is "the unlawful use, act, or threat of violence by a group or individual to advance a social or religious ideology, belief, or cause through intimidation or coercion of the government in the pursuit of political change." Governments have used proxy countries and governments for generations to distance themselves from involvement in global conflicts. Proxy governments are associated with the host government, but simultaneously, the host government can plead plausible deniability [30] for their proxy's actions. For example, North Korea receives its funds from China, and Syria receives its funds from Russia. While this list goes on, these host groups claim innocence for criminal acts done by their proxies by denying responsibility for them due to a lack of evidence connecting them to these events. Meanwhile, proxy governments are used to develop weapons, create disruptions, spy, and conduct evil acts. In contrast, the host government maintains that the proxy government acts independently and of its own accord.

When discussing who and what a terrorist or terrorist organization is, we have to examine today's events and determine what meets the criteria for terrorism. We must look at the totality of the circumstances that cause the events to be dubbed "a terrorist act." For example, many will argue that the Black Lives Matter movement is a domestic terrorist organization. But is it? Again, we take a look at the totality of the circumstances, and today, this points us in a new direction and definition of domestic terrorism.

With Proxyism, acts of terrorism are carried out through a subset group or proxy to act on the other's behalf, which maintains and creates a separation from the host group. Proxyism allows these subsets to use the same movement or platform to carry out terrorist acts. These may include bombing, arson, kidnapping and ransoms, skyjacking, hijacking, murder and assassination, maiming, ambushes, and now, rioting, or other unlawful crimes involving violence as a primary source of coercion. The significance of the identification of Proxyism is critical for movements to be held accountable for their actions. Proxyism differs from the existing crime of conspiring in one significant way – Government coercion.

Distancing oneself from committing a crime or conducting unlawful violence on one's behalf is not new. The difference between Proxyism and conspiring to commit crimes is located directly in the agreement and intended result -- of perceived personal gain. Conspiring was the way Al Capone maintained his innocence as a man. One-minute, Capone was operating soup kitchens for the poor in his neighborhood, and the next, he was conspiring and utilizing organized crime to carry out murder and intimidation. Al Capone received the people's support because of the false moral platform upheld by feeding the poor and helping the needy in his neighborhood. Capone was careful to maintain separation between his good deeds and the violent acts he facilitated. Although directly and indirectly responsible for hundreds of deaths[31], Capone was never convicted of murder; he was only convicted of mail fraud, tax evasion, and probation violations because his two contrasting lives were so well disassociated. The difference between Al Capone's conspiring to commit crimes and today's Proxyism, again, is that Proxyism is the motivation of committing criminal acts to coerce the government, versus Capone's reasoning of projected personal gain.

★★★★

Terrorism or Not?

People often assume a tragic event with mass casualties is terrorism, but this is not true. What is the difference between the right-wing domestic terrorist, Timothy McVeigh, and the Las Vegas music festival shooter, Steven Paddock? Both used violence on the public on a grand scale planned for the attack and carried out their deranged plans with devastating effects. The difference was in motivation and purpose. McVeigh had political aims[32] while he sought revenge against the federal government for the 1993 Waco siege that ended in the deaths of 86 people, many of whom were children, the 1992 Ruby Ridge siege, and for its foreign policy. He hoped to inspire a revolution against the federal government and defended the bombing as a legitimate tactic against what he saw as a tyrannical government. Paddock, in contrast, had no political agenda. His act was that of a deranged mass murderer. While these individuals created horrific and unspeakable events with the loss of many lives, the aim to decrease potential terrorist and non-terrorist acts has become a key priority in cities and states across the country.

★★★★

Negotiating with Domestic Terrorism

Like all other roots of terrorism, there is no exception in trying to negotiate with domestic terrorists acting through Proxyism. One example I have learned through examining Proxyism is that any demands made are a red herring and bear no actual impact on resolving the issues. The masses cannot be appeased, and any attempts to negotiate are futile. These criminals have an immediate goal of clandestine anarchy destructiveness in any form, masked behind a shield of masks and anonymity. The rioters will end when they decide their veil of anonymity is fading. Submission to diversionary demands begets more elaborate, illogical demands. This is an endless cycle that promotes terrorism to achieve a social or political goal by baiting authorities into perceived "non-compliance" with demands. Even if demands are met in one situation, terrorists can always push for more, knowing that you will inevitably cower, and all they have to do is wait. We see this issue today with political leaders governing states and allowing their cities to burn. By public leaders taking zero steps to enforce the law and foolheartedly entertaining one-sided negotiations and demands, they essentially permit businesses to be destroyed for the sake of appeasing an unappeasable, angry mob. Hoping the violent acts will stop on their own accord after meeting demands is merely wishful thinking. These politicians hope to gain the support of the masses, but they are also causing problems for their political aspirations. Still, they also lack the purpose required to solve the crisis at hand urgently. As Princeton University historian Julian Zelizer states, "In the absence of presidential leadership, and with crowds gathering yet again, members of Congress, governors, and mayors need to step up. [33] Good leaders cannot separate themselves from the turbulence. If they're silent, or if they're too distant, it just adds to the frustration people feel."

International negotiations are no different. The U.S. experienced this during their negotiation efforts with the Taliban after 9/11. Even during the peace negotiations, the Taliban continued to carry out its attacks while American and Afghan forces suffered significant losses. certain domestic and international terrorist groups and individuals are called extremists for a reason. They do not have a clue of capacity or desire to negotiate as they proceed with their violent, inhumane, and rampant destruction.

★★★★

Components of Proxyism

Listed below are the **components** and *characteristics* when Proxyism occurs:

1. Some, but not all, of the host group's skepticism of public organizations or government is valid and supported. They wish to gain moral superiority in the public's eye.

2. The host group desires to see disruption, defunding, or destruction of public organizations that play an indispensable role in society and present as an easy target for public social backing due to a common theme.

3. The removal of obstacles through "perceived public outrage" that impede ideological progression is an on-going goal and must be maintained to wear down opponents and public leadership.

4. The demonstration or use of non-sequitur, or distracting issues, when met with resistance, is used to sidetrack logical arguments and fuel their social backing.

5. Both sides of the debate have perceived merit, but oppositional views are disregarded, diminished, or ignored.

6. The host group tends to oversimplify topics and promote a "with us or against us" format for debate.

7. Groups manipulate public support through Stockholm Syndrome or falsely project ethics to gain support and rationalization for their cause and effect.

8. Violence, or collateral damage to private and public property, is attributed to resistance and an acceptable result to challenging the host group.

★★★★

	Leadership Traits
Host Group Leadership Traits	Here is a list of traits you will typically see within the largest or *host group's* leadership: • Advocates a vision that is highly discrepant from the status-quo. • Acts in unconventional ways. • Demonstrates self-sacrifices. • Has confidence in one's objectives and ability to create change. • Takes responsibility or justifies their actions based on internal characteristics. • Uses public persuasive appeals, rather than authority or a structured decision process. • Uses capacity to access or develop context, create an uneven playing field, and locate opportunities through public confusion and anger.
	Leadership Traits
Proximal Subset Group (Parasitic)	Proxyism *leadership traits* tend to follow blaming or situational attribution for circumstances that are perceived to be out of their control as a justification of their behavior. • Blame their behavior on the situation, rather than an internal characteristic. • Deflect or redirect responsibility. • Actions are unpredictable and opportunistic, and do not have a pattern based on personal or group ethics or morals. • Not conforming to social norms or expectations. • Non-socially desirable actions create contempt or feelings of exclusion. • Take credit for what is perceived to be liked by the group and displace blame for what is not liked, regardless of direct involvement.

Group Traits

The subset group or proxy group assisting in the host group's movement is influenced directly by the often-poor leadership it receives. The subset group can many times be a "fly by the seat of your pants" group, or a "hasty" group, pulled together spontaneously, and without any preparation, planning, or resources.

These groups often contain the following attributes:

- Competition [*storming*] among leadership is constant.
- Intergroup conflict is common.
- Leadership vs. followership and roles are unclear and questioned [*conforming*].
- Confusion prevents positive group dynamics [*norming*] from happening.
- An "in or out" mentality encourages conforming.
- Rush to judgment and impulsive decisions.
- Perception of leadership is questioned consistently.
- Conflicting ideas and organizational direction from subordinate members are suppressed with threats of violence or expulsion from the group.
- Frequency of interaction between leadership and subordinates is limited.
- Scarce resources (e.g., hand-drawn signs vs. preprinted and organized propaganda).
- Ambiguity and meaningless work assignments to group members display a facade of control or direction that does not support or promote the advancement of the group or cause.
- Avoidance of dealing with problems within the group.
- Overcompensating with extortion or violence because they do not possess the forbearance to resolve issues or defiance constructively.
- Conflict of morals, goals, ethics, within their group.
- Complete lack of planning, direction, or attainable goals.
- Scenarios become akin to "the blind leading the blind".
- Confined operational space or unable to expand due to lack of buy-in or internal group demise.

Proximal Subset Group (Parasitic)

169

Terrorism and Insurance Providers

It is essential to discuss why labeling something as a terrorist act or not has a significant effect on the public. Once a government labels an act as terrorism, the government sets various funds and responses from agencies, such as FEMA, to aid in recovery and claims into motion. Many people do not know that when the government declares a terrorist act, their private insurance or business insurance no longer openly takes sole responsibility for paying claims related to the incident. Personal insurance companies, such as life insurance policies, often place a clause in the fine print or have disclaimers that void the policy in acts of war, acts of God, and yes, acts of terrorism. For example, local business owners may face significant challenges to rebuild their damaged or destroyed stores because of this clause.

It is in the best interest of all individuals and businesses to review their policies and file or renew their policy with a terrorism addendum, typically at an additional cost. As an emergency manager, your relationship with the individuals and local businesses is one of trust. When speaking with the public or businesses about building resiliency within the community, be sure to address this issue and make it known. You can even go the extra mile and contact a list of insurance providers that require the addendum and prepare a handout for local businesses at public meetings. While insurance companies are happy to assist, from time to time, there are instances when the fine print of what insurance companies will and will not cover is changed and brought to your attention. Your proactive support for business owners will help in case of a tragic event. Your actions will show that you are looking out for your community and have a good understanding of the many detailed facets your job asks and requires of you. If insurance companies deny your community's claims for help, you better believe they will be overwhelming you soon after that for answers and assistance. As an emergency manager, you will also need to have an action plan where local business owners approach you requesting help amid their challenges.

Even during domestic terror incidents, the emergency manager's mission never changes; it just expands. As events occur, the emergency manager accepts the size and scope, and learns to adapt, pivot, adjust, and continue learning. Just like preparing for a hurricane, the basic needs of people and the environment don't change. When a city faces riots, a shooting, or any other violent act or threat, the emergency manager still needs to assess the level of complexity and urgency of the situation and move to act accordingly. Anticipating whether the event—and more specifically, a hurricane—will be a category one or a category four will dictate just how much and how long we need to prepare.

Prioritizing domestic threats has come to the forefront of our country's precedence. Domestic terror arrests were nearly equal [34] to the number of international terror arrests in the first three quarters of 2019. Whether the threat is jihadist or right-wing extremist, emergency managers need to be prepared with manpower, funding, equipment, and resources and to be ready to take action to protect and preserve our people and homeland.

★★★★

CHAPTER 7

FEMA'S CYCLE OF EMERGENCY MANAGEMENT

The Missing Link

For decades, FEMA has relied upon and taught the same model with the four steps of preparedness, response, recovery, and mitigation, but with *no* changes to it in decades. Even with new threats emerging and new emergency events occurring, these steps have not been updated, nor has there been any new guidance or new methodologies to meet these modern-day problems head-on. Especially if you are new to the emergency management field and are just being introduced to the forefront and staple of emergency management training, you will learn what's been in place forever. The current federal policy is still dependent upon a simple cycle in their manuals for years. Whether used for a hurricane, food shortage, a terrorist bombing, or another kind of emergency event, the same model is executed. But as you can imagine, using the same diluted solution for different problems is very limiting and can only get you so far.

★★★★

The issue with this lack of innovation is that it has been enough for FEMA just to get by. However, its general labels and lack of adjustments or advancements allow failure to be repeated with less-than-desirable results. It is the equivalent of "government cheese" for directions. Yes, it technically fulfills the intended purpose, but you may not want to use it on your sandwich if something better is available. Once in a while, someone has added an extra arrow or step to the model, such as training, but even with dozens of extra steps, this continues a broken cycle with an extra element, which only prolongs results. And in these scenarios, the additions made attempting to cater its strategies to a specific type of emergency event only works for that event and not others. The current FEMA model is in dire need of including a step in reflecting upon what worked and what did not. What also needs greater attention is the opportunities and platforms to share and distribute newly discovered strategies and practices that worked! Without these, many emergency managers and emergency management teams are shortsighted and have a deficiency of resources at their fingertips. This is not ideal, considering how significant emergency management plays its role in protecting millions of people in public safety, public health, and disaster management.

Even when the cycle and its policies create unsuccessful outcomes, I have found that this is continually blamed on an increasing operational gap year over year— meaning the policy was in place but not updated as leadership changed hands over and over. Still, there was no one hired or appointed to update, uphold, or enforce it. Similar to when a new president of the United States takes office: the shortfalls are often blamed on their predecessor, having laid the groundwork for the failure. As senior management moves out of position, new management continues to utilize what was already in place from the past until they put their vision in place – or don't. While it is understandably challenging to amend policies, akin to changing the direction of a ship at sea with little power, it is critical to do so—especially when these policies bring about a lack of preparedness and leave the public's safety in jeopardy and with poor results. As a new emergency manager, you may inherit a handful of plans that sets into place for the sake of "checking the box" for management that, for lack of a better term, are generally outdated and useless. This cycle is equal to something as simple as the directions on a shampoo bottle: wet hair, lather, rinse, repeat. In our very real-world safety threats to the American people across its towns and cities, emergency management's current state follows simple steps that continue not to work: fail, blame, leave, repeat. Simplicity is great, and many can recall the four steps of the FEMA cycle. Still, when people do not know how to apply it or innovate and revise when necessary, it becomes just another on-going problem in solving problems.

Trying to use the same tool to fix all the various problems comes to mind when I view this short cycle. There is an old saying, "When you are a hammer, every problem looks like a nail," which holds here. Starting with this cycle is a great place to begin, and there is nothing wrong with that. But it's still barely enough to lead and guide managers and teams when emergencies happen and reinforce preliminary plans as acceptable. Especially as there's been a shift in the kinds of emergencies we have been facing and experiencing, even just this year, this model also runs parallel to this example: Imagine what would happen if you referred to a basic car manual for different cars' models. This, in theory, should work! Our world has been driving gasoline-powered vehicles for more than a century. But in 2020, with the electrification of transportation increasing globally, in the U.S., if you pull into an auto shop with an electric car, such as a Tesla, the manual for vehicles with an internal combustion engine no longer applies. Even as it shares the same function as a gas-powered car, an electric car is an entirely new product with a completely different manual vital to figuring out its unique needs, issues, and solutions. Yes, the original manual worked for a very long time, but it can only be helpful when it is no longer relevant for all cars. Frequently FEMA's cycle is shortsighted to add any new parts and not thorough enough actually to execute steps to improve outcomes and results. Something needs to be refashioned for this cycle to stop finally. Do you see something similar happening in your department? What steps can you take to move your agency away from regular cycles that have proved they are not precisely the solution you need?

The government was not fashioned to generate or create innovative change. The government is built to fund outside contracted sources that develop innovative change. It depends on these third parties to get a crucial job done, but unfortunately, this work does not always get done, and many times, these third parties find they have severe limitations to what they can do in scope.

★★★★

The number of rules and regulations stating what federal criminal offenses are is now in the 300,000s. This continues to grow since old and outdated laws are not removed, including antiquated laws related to Indian Tribes and unshaken laws that further spur civil rights movements in 2020. [35] Instead of creating and adding laws we desperately need and repealing out-dated laws no longer relevant in today's society [36], the collection grows. This list has now become unmanageable, overwhelming, and includes nonsensical laws. One example of a jailable offense is walking your dog on federal grounds with a leash that is longer than six feet will land you in prison. Even at the state-level, [37], ridiculous examples of unrepealed laws include playing pinball if you are under 18-years of age, requiring pickles to bounce, throwing a ball at another person's face during a dodgeball game, and talking and moving a rake from New Jersey into New York. These are real, and I am not kidding.

During the coronavirus pandemic, the American president was criticized for hesitating to immediately employ a Korean War-era law called the Defense Production Act. [38] Designed to push federal orders first in line so companies could focus on the country's specific procurement of vital equipment. This pandemic did not initially seem to bring the same urgency as the 300,000 times this law was used by the president this past year. The Department of Defense stated that the Defense Production Act was tapped into to "build lasers, jet engines, and armored vehicles," but had yet to be utilized to save the hundreds of thousands of American lives at stake with the incredibly contagious virus. The president finally decided to use the Defense Production Act. On April 16th, 2020, GM and Ventec Life Systems finally delivered 30,000-units of life-saving ventilators[39] to hospitals across the country that needed them the most. Even when the administration disagreed with the contract price, the two companies moved forward with the ventilators' production to prevent any significant delays from occurring. The contract was ultimately finalized. This law has been activated many times for many reasons, and one our country needs during challenging times. Having this law in place enables us to use it as a game-changer during a crisis our nation faces, but only if executed and promptly employed by the administration.

★★★★

In the wake of the Black Lives Matter movement and other "social justice" movements this year, police reform has become an on-going headline across the country. When the necessary, everyday activities of the police force are remarked by the public as unclear, undocumented, and do not even exist in many departments, regulating practices takes a lot more effort, groundwork, refining, and, yes, **funding.** [40]

This brings us back to the question of defunding the police force when precisely the opposite may be necessary. Ensuring sufficient resources will be available to train police departments, successfully revise policies, provide proper supervision and internal investigations, and place significant administrative reviews key to getting many police forces back on track. Perhaps defunding should only be a part of the conversation when specific departments are misallocating funds irresponsibly and not carrying out the duties to serve their communities the way they should. While state legislatures can move much more quickly than Congress can, even looking into one area like police reform, you can get a glimpse of why it's so difficult to see real transformation happen. The same can be said in numerous fields related to and including emergency management.

Since cited powers [41] limit the federal government, it can only execute power granted by the U.S. constitution. Then, states have a much more flexible time exercising the authority given to them without running into constitutional fences. The federal government's structural and systematic deficiency is a worthy cause for ill-improved procedures, policies, and unsuccessful consequences and aftereffects.

★★★★

Looking back a bit further to 9/11, we can see how new terrorist challenges overtook the U.S. and seemed to single-handedly dismantle national security on all levels. Although unpredictable and unprecedented events like 9/11 can seemingly shake our country to its core, reorganizing and sharpening security after such an incredulous time as this ought to be of the utmost priority. However, disappointingly enough, several years later, after 9/11, the country didn't seem any more prepared for potential future attacks than it was when the devastating events happened in 2001. Questions about intelligence spending, higher quality communication systems for first responders and detainees' handling continued, and progress remained doubtful. Somehow, air travelers' identities within the U.S. were not diligently and carefully watched, and questionable funds were being disbursed to parts of the country that were at shallow risk of any terrorist attack.

The former Republican governor of New Jersey, Thomas H. Kean, who had served as chairman of the September 11th panel, stated, "Four years after 9/11, we are not as safe as we could be, and that's simply not acceptable. While the terrorists are learning and adapting, our government is still moving at a crawl." [42] Just the thought of our government not being able to keep up with those trying to overtake us can quickly instill a sense of uneasiness and anxiety for us citizens, especially when we already know we are vulnerable. Of course, we'd expect our country's leaders to be ahead of the game and be prepared for whatever event will come our way. We still expect this of them today, and we should.

By two decades after 9/11, hundreds of billions of dollars had been spent, and a complete reorganization of federal agencies had taken place. We would want to believe that, at that point, the country was in much better shape to handle any type of domestic or foreign terrorist attack. Still, assessments say otherwise. Again, recommendations were made by the National Commission on Terrorist Attacks Upon the United States. And sadly, processes to coordinate rescues, effective communication systems for emergency responders, and the ability to detect explosives on planes were still inadequate and unreliable. With these kinds of reports, it's incredible that citizens continued to fly and travel as much as they did. In the *Tenth Anniversary Report Card: The Status of 9/11 Commission Recommendations,* the panel found that there were still weak security requirements for people who attempted to obtain identity cards, and shockingly, Congress had still not yet passed a law to issue first responders a dedicated radio spectrum. These recommendations were directly given due to critical failures experienced during 9/11, and it is mind-boggling to see how suggestions are either not made, even after one decade, or ignored. [43]

★★★★

Continuing to take routes with unsuccessful outcomes reminds me of my time in the Marine Corps. We had a saying, *"Do as you have always done; get what you have always got."* This is a pretty straightforward and accurate quote with a lot of truth to it. It encompasses the issues surrounding complacency and settling for the bare minimum as *acceptable* in any given situation. It is also a loose representation of the definition of insanity. In other words, don't be surprised by the outcome if you are approaching a specific problem the very same way that led you to failure. There is nothing wrong with a repeating cycle if it is complete, it works, and it gives you the flexibility to break the cycle because something better has introduced itself. There needs to be a development or break-out that makes the cycle more of a spiral than that of a circle, or possibly a modified infinity symbol to create more opportunities to revamp, innovate, and solve emergencies more constructively than ever before.

★★★★

CHAPTER 8

RAND'S GOLDEN RULE
(Of 8's or 'ates')

Breaking the old patterns

Here is a summary of FEMA's emergency management cycle today—the same one that has existed for years and has not changed: Preparedness, Response, Recovery, Mitigation. These are the descriptions given, by FEMA, on what to do for each phase. This is *it*.

Model: FEMA Cycle [44]

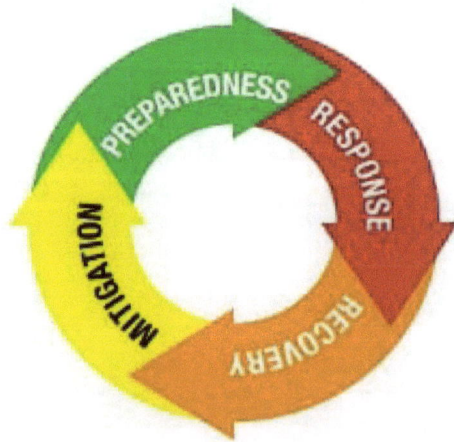

Mitigation   This phase includes any activities that prevent an emergency, reduce the likelihood of occurrence, or reduce the damaging effects of unavoidable hazards. Mitigation activities should be considered long before an emergency.

Preparedness   This phase includes developing plans for what to do, where to go, or who to call for help before an event occurs; actions that will improve your chances of successfully dealing with an emergency.

Response   Your safety and well-being in an emergency depend on how prepared you are and on how you respond to a crisis. By being able to act responsibly and safely, you will be able to protect yourself, your family, others around you and your animals.

Recovery   After an emergency and once the immediate danger is over, your continued safety and well-being will depend on your ability to cope with rearranging your life and environment. During the recovery period, you must take care of yourself and your animals to prevent stress-related illnesses and

With a new cycle I created from scratch, I wanted to design something that could be flexible enough to cater to any emergency event planning and follow practical and reliable steps.

In *Rand's Golden Rule of 8s*, the eight steps are: Initiate, Formulate, Incorporate, Articulate, Innovate, Mandate, and Educate. Within these steps, every person involved in the cycle is empowered to think through preventative or problem-solve. Then, these ideas can be shared and tested before mandating, educating, and disseminating them. It is vital to alter operations and steps and create a modified, customized cycle for emergency events that come our way. And at some point, I'm aware that this cycle is not absolute, but it allows for greater efficiency, improvements, and productivity.

Innovating is all about discovering a better way to do something. Disseminating this is finding a solution in Washington D.C. and sharing this solution with a city in Wisconsin that could use it effectively for its communities. Dissemination is vital because others may benefit from innovative approaches, tactics, and practices they were unaware of until it was shared. A centralized hub where all towns and cities, no matter how small or large, can draw solutions to best help their population is needed in emergency management today. Emergency managers, and everyone involved in tackling emergencies, could use a place where a collection of techniques and best practices are shared, so no one is starting. But instead, they can utilize valuable and shared resources in the most advantageous way possible.

A cycle allowing more people to participate in it and provide more significant innovation to solve today's complex emergencies is critical to our country staying a few steps ahead of the issues. Having a trustworthy model where you can break out and innovate and test ideas out before executing them is essential for successful emergency management outcomes. This is what I believe is the missing link in the emergency management planning of 2021.

★★★★

Rand's 'Golden Rule of 8s"

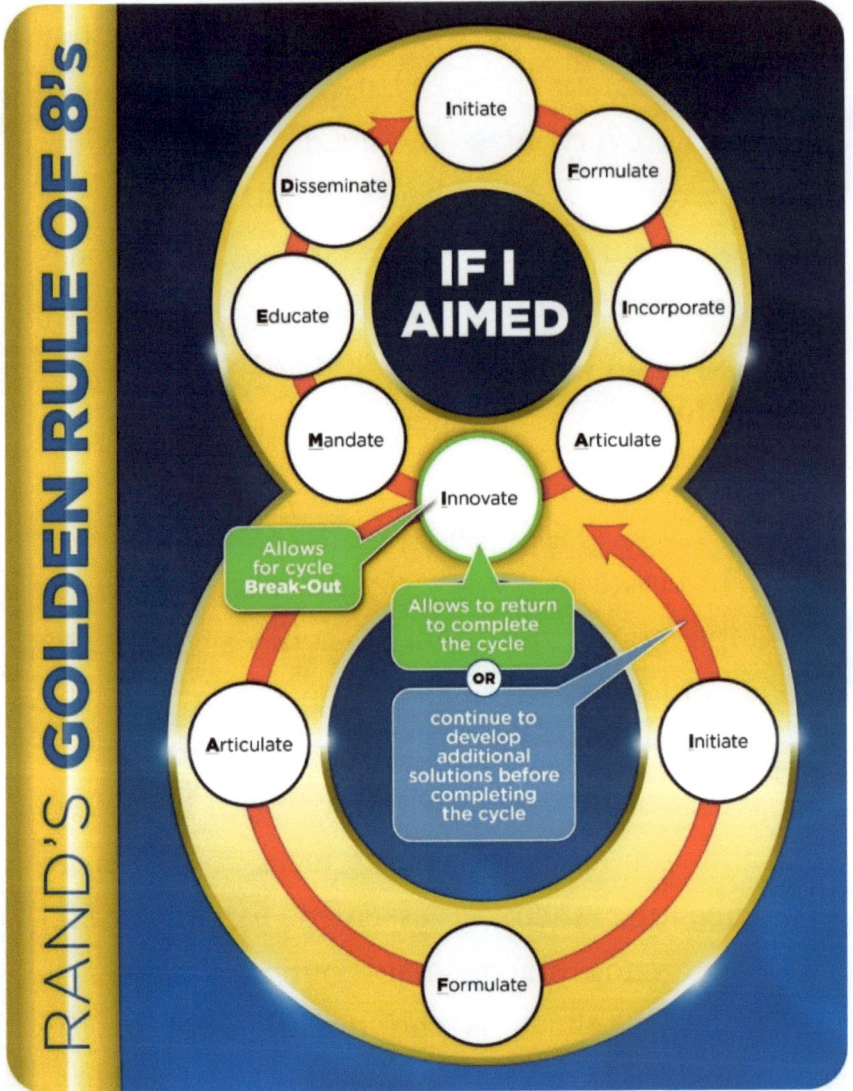

All adequate planning procedures follow a path that is easy to remember, and my golden Rule of Eights is no different. Take a look at the list below for a new spin on the planning process and the ability to innovate and still complete the planning cycle. It's the refresher that FEMA's cycle so desperately needs to move forward and adapt to the changing world:

★★★★

ACRONYM:

"I.F. I. A.I.M.E.D"

1. Initiate:

Begin the Planning Process.

Every plan has to start somewhere. Initiating the planning process for the issue you have uncovered is more than just ready, set, go! When you initiate the planning process, you must identify what issues you are addressing, who needs to be involved, what resources you may require, and who you need to reach with your information.

★★★★

2. **F**ormulate:

Establish your purpose.

When you formulate a plan, you must take in all of the relevant factors and the totality of the circumstances to ensure a complete plan from start to finish. The easiest way to accomplish this goal is to create an outline by arranging your topics to ensure the items you have identified in your initiation are present and ensure your plan makes logical sense and provides a clear path to your goal.

★★★★

3. Incorporate:

Make objectives and goals to fulfill your purpose.

Now that you have identified all of your required topics for your outline begin going through your support agreements and your existing resources to find out where they will fall into your plan. If something is missing, figure out the best way to acquire it, whether it be lease, purchase, borrow, etc. Incorporate the groups, departments, political figures, outside agencies, or members that need to be included for the plan to be successful.

★★★★

4. Articulate:

Be able to express your ideas to leadership clearly.

As mentioned in the previous item, you must adequately professionally speak about the topic and address all questions that may arise. If you cannot clearly articulate what you set out to do, you will not get or achieve buy-in from political figures, department heads, or other stakeholders that provide the means for you to accomplish your goal. Practice your pitch in private, from start to finish, and anticipate any questions in advance, so you can adequately answer them with the correct information. Once you have done this a time or two, you will see these questions often remain the same from issue to issue. Many leaders want to know how it will impact them personally, the agency financially, or the legalities or liabilities your plan may present.

5. Innovate:

Your goals should establish a new benchmark standard.

They arise before completing your planning process. In other words, it is essential to have a breaking-off point that allows you to apply your knowledge, experience, and skill to conquer an issue in a way that previous individuals may not have attempted. When you have discovered a way to eliminate an issue that others have not, it is essential for there to be a way to share your knowledge.

★★★★

6. <u>M</u>andate:

Leadership must authorize the authority to implement.

When you have completed your plan, the next step is to address those in charge again, receive the go-ahead, and put your plan into action. A plan is only a plan until there is an authority behind it to ensure the plan is carried out correctly. This authority is achieved by addressing all involved and implementing a direct executive order to enforce the plan.

★★★★

7. **E**ducate:

Train, test, and evaluate all involved.

All individuals, agencies, groups, and departments must know what they expect to accomplish this goal. This can only be done by educating all those involved with the complete plan, especially your innovation(s) and how it leads to the successful culmination of the entire planning process. Only then can you expect the operational component of the plan to be effective and carried out correctly.

★★★★

8. Disseminate:

Ensure that all jurisdictions receive your plan.

Regardless of your plan's outcome, you must be willing to disseminate all information in your After-Action Report (AAR) to all those involved and all those who could be involved in the future. You must memorialize this information so your successes are documented, and your failures will not be repeated. Sometimes, pride must take a backseat when your plan does not work out as you anticipated. Even though you do not consider failure as an attribute, it is still vital information that helps others avoid mistakes and innovate a new way to help make your plan and thrive in the future. Too often, people hide their failures and do not allow others to learn from them to benefit the greater good.

★★★★

CHAPTER 9

GROUP DYNAMICS

Intro

When I think of group dynamics, I cannot help but compare it to one of John Hughes's classic '80s movies, *The Breakfast Club*. You see, whenever you get a group of people together, they naturally begin to form cliques, gravitate toward like-individuals and distance themselves from those they find nothing in common with. Each character in *The Breakfast Club* represents different society members who are forced to spend time together in a confined space and learn to deal with each other's quirks and annoyances. Real-life group dynamics are not far from this at all, which is why the movie is so funny and touches members of all age groups and socioeconomic backgrounds. It's why the show "The Office" works—it's why people watch it and say, "You remind me of so-and-so," or, "So-and-so is like this person." Group dynamics don't change because it is fundamental human nature. However, rather than saying, "This person is the 'idiot' of the group," we do have to use a bit more decorum.

★★★★

Defining Group Dynamics

What are group dynamics? Only it is is human interaction. Whether within the same group or between groups, group dynamics studies how groups are formed, structured, and function. Let's start with family. We are all born into a family and into a dynamic that we learn to process, understand, incorporate ourselves in, and function within. Everyone has a family and finds themselves growing up among a core group of people—whether with parents, grandparents, siblings, extended relatives, or even non-familial persons who play a role, however minimal or significant. While each person has a unique perspective on their own family's group dynamics, we can all say we have one. Typically, with the first group dynamics we ever experience in life, we come to know its structure, how things usually play out within it, who plays which role, and how okay families function as a whole. There will be recurring themes and dynamics that perhaps you wish you could change and others you cherish, agree with, and see as ideal.

★★★★

Leadership in Police Organizations discusses the cohesion theory, which is defined as "the degree to which members are attracted to and remain in a group." In group dynamics, the stronger the cohesion that exists, the more likely you will find these traits: [45]

- Mutual respect
- Trust
- Confidence
- Understanding
- Performance
- Achieving goals
- Open communication channels
- Accepted feedback
- Willingness to sacrifice
- Higher tolerance towards external stress, pressure, influence
- Loyalty and satisfaction

In turn, higher levels of care, commitment, energy, and collective resources your group will gain due to positive and higher levels of cohesion. To facilitate, nurture, and organize a new group of people—however many there are—and well-built foster cohesion is the end goal for you as an emergency manager.

★★★★

Individuals are influenced by various mediums, including peers, media, entertainment, music, current news, aspirations, motivations, and needs. But all of these viewpoints depend on the psyche, make-up, and outlook of each person in the picture. How often are families successful in reaching goals together, holding the same vision, or managing different worldviews, opinions, and priorities? I think it's safe to say that most of us have experienced that in our own families, where the average number in an American family is two. [46] It may seem impossible to cooperate, agree to disagree, and remain in unity and as a team in many cases. The overlay of human behavior in any group—whether within family, sports teams, riots, movements, or companies—is merely another place group dynamics form, just with varied numbers of individuals and greater diversity in individuals' walks of life and communication styles.

★★★★

How people work within these settings is related to their moral relativism, which is mainly shaped by culture and society. As moral relativism has become a reality and has a more significant presence in American society, people's challenge to understand beliefs and values different from their own does not always play out smoothly. While all of us need to be aware of where the next person is coming from and why they believe what they believe, this is not always achieved, and things do not always go as perfectly as we'd like. In facing group dynamics within the emergency management setting, you are usually playing the cards you're dealt with, no matter who is on your team or in the group you're directing, and your own ability to manage group dynamics will be critical to your success.

In my situation, I've found that what I've learned in the past is coming true. People do jockey for power and position. One way to measure how prepared a person is to take up a new role, whether as a volunteer or emergency manager, is to see their record as followers. While leadership cannot exist without at least one follower, you will find that good leaders' characteristics are also found in excellent followers. When you are recruiting to fill roles, ask yourself if this person is proactive rather than passive. Is this person known for their hard work? Superior leaders and followers exhibit independence, critical thinking, and innovation. Think, "This person is thorough and creative in obtaining the resources, information, and skills that are needed to do the job... the interpersonal dynamics of the workplace are not a primary concern."

★★★★

Workplaces are set, and you have your designated spot where everyone can find you, and likewise, you know where to go to find who you need. Similarly, in emergency shelters, people find themselves temporarily stuck together with people they never met

14

before. This can go on for a while. Where you have people, you have group dynamics, and understanding the dynamics within an emergency shelter requires good judgment, quick decision-making, and an ability to interact with people in such a way that you can rapidly reveal the core of who they are in the time you have.

I've worked with so many groups and people through the years and have always found theories and group dynamics applications to help an emergency manager. Here are several theories and their applications that can be vital for you in your role as emergency manager:

★★★★

Maslow's Hierarchy of Needs

In 1943, Abraham Maslow, an American psychologist, introduced a hierarchy of needs in a paper and in a book he wrote subsequently. Maslow believed people were motivated by five factors at varying degrees, and his theory is portrayed as a pyramid diagram, such as the one below. Maslow's theory caught the attention of many and is still influential today. Because of the typical route of pinpointing illnesses and abnormalities, Maslow's approach was to search for ways to help people become happier, feel more whole, be more self-aware, and experience greater satisfaction in life.

Physiological

Starting at the base of the pyramid are physiological needs. These include food, clothing, water, warmth, and sleep. Maslow believed that these primary needs need to be met before moving up to the pyramid's next steps. People are mainly driven to achieve these needs as a priority and above everything else.

Security and Safety

The next level of needs that Maslow believed motivated and propelled people to action was safety and security. This could be referring to financial stability, having a home or shelter, one's health and well-being, and not being in a situation that left one vulnerable or exposed to accidents or injuries, whether physically, mentally, or psychologically. Driven by the need for safety and security, people may take steps to secure a home or health insurance, contribute to their savings account, or move down the road to living on a safer street.

Social

The next level of Maslow's hierarchy of needs is people's need to feel accepted and loved. This social need speaks to the emotional relationships people have through family, friendships, romantic relationships, and groups they belong to. Meeting this social need allows people to thrive relationally, emotionally, and psychologically. It also keeps individuals from experiencing isolation, loneliness, and depression.

Esteem

The esteem level is when individuals are motivated by respect and appreciation, and as a result, have their self-esteem and self-worth boosted. Many people will have these needs met by reaching specific goals, accomplishments, and achievements, such as completing a degree, running a marathon, or learning a new skill. The esteem and social levels are known to be the psychological needs of Maslow's hierarchy.

Self-actualization

At the peak of Maslow's hierarchy pyramid is self-actualization. Maslow believed that the ultimate way for people to motivate themselves was in the process of reaching one's potential. While this could be equated to finding success, Maslow believed that "what a man can be, he must be." [47] Whether this was through one's personality, resources, talent, skills, or performance, what nearly drove people to greatness would be to attain self-actualization. This reminds me of the U.S. Army's long-running slogan, "Be all that you can be." If we help individuals be everything they can become, we are on track to seeing them succeed, find reasons to act, and take action.

★★★★

To be clear, there's no strict order in which people will move through the levels of Maslow's hierarchy of needs. Specific individuals will have the social or esteem needs as their base level and will seek connection or acceptance, placing this need even before food and shelter at times. Others will have the safety level take precedence over the other levels of the pyramid. It's your job as emergency manager to be aware of these levels, as you work with a wide array of individuals, and to be mindful of them when interacting with them and making decisions on their behalf.

★★★★

Group Dynamics Cycle:

Forming, Storming, Norming, Performing, and Adjourning

The forming, storming, norming, and performing model was created by psychologist Bruce Tuckman and introduced in an article he wrote in 1965. I'd like to include his theory in this chapter since it applies every time you, as an emergency manager, are tasked to work with a new group during a new disaster. After explaining each of its fundamental aspects, it's also vital to see how applications can be made in real scenarios and events. [48]

Forming

Forming is the introductory stage when a new group of strangers meets a specific set of goals. In this phase, you will establish clear objectives, develop a group's baseline, and understand who has entered the group dynamic. Knowing people will naturally react differently to a new scenario. You will quickly need to be aware of individuals' types and manage them best. It's crucial that once the norms are established, opportunities are not given to the group to overpower the leader and remove them from the position.

The duration of the forming stage can vary quite a bit. As an emergency manager, your leadership and position are critical in forming since everyone else's role is clear or defined. People will look to you for direction, try to create direction, or lack motivation. As the emergency manager, you must comprehend the who, what, and whys of the situation and delegate while making decisions accordingly.

Storming

Storming is, yes, the stormy stage. During storming, individuals start to test out their roles and, in the process, begin to find that their personalities, outlooks, or working styles clash with those within the group. People can become complacent, competitive, frustrated, or burdened with a high percentage of the workload. All sorts of things can happen within storming. As the emergency manager, you will help iron out others' roles and differences and align the group with its original purpose and goals. As a leader in this process, you understand why people are doing or saying things and continue to layout processes, procedures, and expectations. Individuals learn more about each other and learn how to function as one entity.

Creating structure, processes, and procedures is vital during storming. Your new group will require substantial guidance as you build trust, model positivity, and coach your team members in assertiveness and conflict resolution skills.

Many groups never get past the storming phase since difficulties of all kinds arise here. Knowing beforehand that storming can get quite rocky, you must identify and delegate tasks and relationships to those who you see becoming instrumental teachers, peacemakers, leaders, and contributors. The strength and skills of specific delegates will help you undertake the storming phase and be ready and prepared to head into the next phase.

Norming

It may be helpful to know leaving the storming phase is never a done deal. Although your group as a whole may now move into the norming phase, any new branch, new task, or new delegation can cause a degree of storming to occur again. Keep this in mind, so you will be prepared for it when it happens.

Congratulations on arriving at the norming phase! During the norming phase, you'll start to see progress made, honest and constructive feedback given and taken, relationships strengthened, and visions line up. As the individuals in your group begin to get to know one another, they will accept one another's differences, form stronger bonds, and show more significant cooperativity and cohesiveness towards their shared activities and goals. During norming, team-building exercises can be helpful, and some will even begin to include each other in their social lives, too. Norming is typically a much more harmonious and calmer stage for you as an emergency manager. People will better understand your role as a leader and will have decided to follow your lead.

Performing

Once you've reached the performing stage with your newly formed group, you have arrived. The performing stage is the ultimate stage to get to for emergency managers. It is here that your group has come to learn each of their defined roles and how to function well within them. The different levels of needs people have are usually met at their highest capacities during the performance. This allows your group to make leaps and bounds towards the goals set before them. As a leader and emergency manager, you will find that you and your group will experience the least amount of friction here. Much of the operations can now be successfully delegated out. At this stage, you will be much more aware of who to delegate to, when to delegate, and how much to allow others to care for. Abundant energy has been spent informing, storming, and norming your group. Performing is the epitome of successful group dynamics reaching its peak, maintaining its output, and even striving towards new pinnacles.

As with any organic and evolving group and its dynamics, there will always be ways to reverse a group's ability to perform. It's crucial to take note of these and watch for them. While any manager would like their group to remain in performing, depending on the event or disaster, that stage is short-term, and all good things are meant to end.

Adjourning

It is often natural for groups to disperse. Look at families: children who grow up into young adults will naturally begin their own families. Sports teams pledge their lives to win championships, but only for a limited number of seasons. College students go to class for only a semester before they conclude, and graduations celebrate the accomplishments of many who are moving onto the beginnings of their careers. Adjourning or mourning is when groups decay, adjourn, or are suspended. This is done for various reasons: a leader is removed, and the group loses vision; organizations are restructured; or when funding is lost, and operations come to a halt. But this happens more often than not, and as an emergency manager, even this final stage is something to prepare for. You may find that you'll work with specific individuals again in the future, so continuing to build on this foundation continues through this stage. Many in the group will gladly move out of their role, but others will find it challenging to have no longer the source that brought them motivation, belonging, and a sense of purpose. Even in this case, your leadership will be significant in supporting those leaving the now-disbanded group.

★★★★

Race for Roles

Anytime you get a group of people together—especially people who do not know each other—that is necessary due to a disaster, or even everyday activities like a college class or extracurricular activity, you can tell a lot by people's behavior the first day you meet them. People need to figure out their roles in a group since this is directly related to their purpose and identity. You will find that falling into roles happens pretty naturally for most people due to personalities and human nature.

In a larger group setting of hundreds of people, it's a good idea to be observant, as there most likely will be smaller cliques within the larger group. Each group figures out their social contract theory and pulls together through commonly shared values and goals. This can quickly transform into advancing a cause and attaining these goals, but it can also give rise to conflict and confrontation. As you deal with smaller groups, the forming, storming, norming, performing, and adjourning/mourning stages will be critical— not only in helping individuals find the best-suited roles to play but also in deciding who is open and willing to support your goals and those who are not.

You will want to consider Maslow's Hierarchy of Needs, even in the context of smaller and larger groups. Maslow's theory is based on how humans behave, so this applies to people within groups of all purposes. For some, belonging to a group will fulfill one or more levels of personal needs. Many individuals who have a shared sense of direction or purpose may be inclined to join groups to feel accepted and belong. This is something to be aware of, and essentially, you will act as a guide to direct and redirect people's hearts, motivations, and needs.

★★★★

As you work with volunteers and civic groups within your community, identifying groups to include in achieving emergency management goals is an excellent place to begin. Depending on the issue at hand and what is going on in the community, you will be prompted to approach organizations such as a church, Rotary Club, Lions Club, or Kiwanis Club. The great thing about civic groups is you'll often find individuals who have a decent degree of experience volunteering for emergencies. Many people I meet through this route already have their focus on their respective communities. Their practical knowledge and experience can be extremely beneficial for those who are brand new.

The art of emergency management in handling group dynamics will depend upon your ability to quickly decipher who individuals indeed are, who's in charge, who will back you, and what current roles are. By picking through the group's pieces, titles aside, you will have to ask questions, even the hard ones. Does this person want a title for their ego? Is this person genuine in their motivation to help out? They say that in business, it is better to be friends with the secretary than the CEO since they'll give you access to everything and already understands what it means to achieve goals by being in a helping role.

★★★★

The emergency manager's role is consistently a challenge. You have to understand people, why they do what they do, and where they're going to fit. You may even need to weed volunteers out if they're acting a certain way that makes you believe they can't be sent out to, for example, a person's house that's been ravaged by a hurricane. Perhaps their character is doubtful or untrustworthy, and due to their motivations, they have the potential to steal, retrieve another person's medication, etc.

When someone is acting counterintuitively, you know something is off; something is wrong. As an emergency manager, it is your job to look out for the people taking advantage of special populations. In some cases, you will have to pick the predator out and, just the same, identify those you can trust to get the job done safely, efficiently, and mindfully. The emergency manager has an abundance of responsibilities within group dynamics. As I have learned, this encompasses skills that can be sharpened with every group you manage and bring through the forming, storming, norming, performing, and adjourning phases.

★★★★

CHAPTER 10

SHELTERING
Dealing with Groups Who Require Special Needs or Protection During an Emergency

Intro

Congratulations! Whether you like it or not, you have just been made mayor of your new makeshift city. The city or county emergency shelter has now been handed over to you like your domain to provide leadership, direction, vision, and operational guidance for hundreds, perhaps even thousands of individuals who've somehow ended up here. All of the responsibilities are now yours—none of the glory—but I repeat, all responsibilities are now on your plate.

Nonetheless, get ready for a whirlwind of issues you are about to face. Emergencies create all sorts of minor and major problems, ranging from life and death situations to providing healthy snacks for young children and elderly seniors. Depending on your level of preparation, planning, exercises, connection to resources, support agreements, mutual aid, information, and personal conflicts, chances are, with all of these demands, you will realize you somehow forgot one essential thing—to run to the restroom. Unfortunately, the one available to you has no toilet paper, and it dawns on you: the absence of toilet paper is on your watch, too.

★★★★

After reading the last chapter on group dynamics and interaction, you should be more familiar with how people interact in social settings. There could not be a better example of group interaction and dynamics than in an emergency sheltering setting. Sheltering situations, regardless of duration or size, will always present the most challenging working environment. It would be best if you on-the-fly had on-the-fly flexibility and organizational skills and the ability to make one of the most challenging decisions in public safety, not helping some people. Let me rephrase that; you will have to reject people from the shelter and send them on their way. That's right, and I did forget to mention one other role of the emergency manager, which is a nightclub bouncer's role. Get used to repeating the phrase, "I'm sorry, but I cannot admit you into this shelter."

Rejecting individuals from the shelter has nothing to do with whether you like the individuals or not. Still, it is based on your duty and responsibility to protect the public and your community's vulnerable populations during times of disaster. You may be the only person standing in the way of a child or elderly person missing meals, lacking medication, or even being abused mentally, physically, or sexually. People will enter into shelters clutching their most prized possessions, only to lose them, and at times, have them stolen—the only personal belongings they have left after a disaster. Being in the emergency manager role requires critical decision-making skills since you will designate who will receive the benefits of residing in the shelter and who will need to find an alternative option after being turned away. Suppose you think about the magnitude of the decisions you will be making. In that case, I bet you will start to see how having this degree of legitimate authority and budget control not only makes a bit more sense and is critical but will directly impact the lives of thousands who are the most in need during emergencies.

★★★★

CHAPTER 11

SPECIAL POPULATIONS

Elderly:

Fortunately, the elderly population is easily identifiable and needs excellent attention during a disaster. The majority of the issues you will face during an emergency will be directed towards caring for the elderly. During and after Hurricane Katrina [49], despite the aged 60 or older group making up only 15-percent of the population of New Orleans, they comprised 75-percent of the individuals found to be deceased during and right after the disaster. Not only do seniors need extra care within the shelters, in case of an evacuation from the emergency shelter, extended [50] plans need to be made to know how they will be removed from the location and where they will go to remain secure.

Seniors will also take up most of the resources you have at hand and require specific resources other groups do not require, such as accessible toilets, hearing aids, scooters, and medication. So, expect this to occur before it does. The elderly demand special resources since each type have unique needs, and frequently, sufficient personnel is mandatory to meet these needs. They may need assistance taking their medication, have special dietary requirements, or require help getting in and out of basic chairs and cots provided in shelters. The needs of seniors usually need to be met for a longer duration than the rest of the population due to their higher percentages of chronic problems. The elderly population presents its unique challenges. These may even encompass several of the other categories of special populations; a few of the major ones include mobility issues, medical issues, and close supervision.

Pets:

Pets are an essential part of our families. Therefore, as emergency managers, we must prepare to shelter family pets, comfort animals, and care for emotional support animals, service animals, and alike. During disasters, thousands of dogs, cats, and other types of pets are displaced and separated from their families. Amid relief efforts, it was found that there was one pet for every two people to track[51] during an emergency. That is a lot of pets to care for! Due to Hurricane Maria, Hurricane Irma, and the Northern California wildfires in 2017, the American Society for the Prevention of Cruelty of Animals (ASPCA) assisted almost 37,000 animals in the latter half of that year. Pets present a significant challenge because, within shelters, even though some will be reunited with their families, they must still be separated from the population and kept in appropriate crates. This doesn't mean families cannot see or interact with them. This procedure protects the mass population from allergic reactions, bites, and other issues, like noise pollution and constant barking and meowing. If you have not had to deal with a pet parent, get ready to experience some friction. Their animal is always the most well-behaved and will not be a problem—until their pet almost always is. Just like for the elderly, emergency preparedness for pets incorporates an impressive list, including things like leashes, daily waste bags, litter and litter boxes, pet food, learning pet CPR, and pet first aid kits.

Foreign Languages:

This is where your familiarity with your community plays a big part. You should be well aware of the cultural sections of your community and the primary languages they speak. During an emergency and on-going emergency such as the coronavirus pandemic, accurate and efficient communication [52] for all individuals can be the difference between life and death. If 50-percent of the limited-English population do not receive translations, there's a good chance 50-percent of those people under your care will not be following the protocols your layout. This is too high of a risk. When those affected by disasters are encouraged to take preventative measures to avoid contamination or be exposed but cannot because they do not grasp the English language, their vulnerability spikes. Even now, with COVID-19 cases rising like never before, there is a disproportionate number of non-English speaking communities being infected and dying.

To prepare for disasters, your interactions with civic groups and churches will give you a suitable generalization of the languages you may encounter in your area. I recommend that you create a roster of volunteers who can serve as interpreters for the languages representing your communities' people. The better and more prompt communication is, the greater the knowledge non-English speakers will obtain regarding their health, healthcare resources, and lifestyle changes in staying safer and healthier. Something as practical as using Google Translate [53] can be used to print out your rules and regulations in the various languages for hundreds, and even thousands, of people who need access to crucial information. However, not 100-percent accurate, [54] using tools like this is a good start and will go a very long way for those who would otherwise be entirely in the dark. Be sure to collaborate with native speakers to confirm that these translations have a high degree of accuracy. Equity and rights in communication, regardless of someone's background, need to be provided with the extra effort and steps required.

Children:

Children typically face multi-layered challenges during a disaster. Caring for children will most likely make up a large percentage of the issues you will manage during an emergency. Since children have not yet developed the mental capacity to understand what is happening or the extent of what is going on, surviving a disaster can be life-changing and create trauma. [55] After going through a significant crisis, children can experience years of psychological aftereffects—such as regressing old habits, having personality changes, and changing sleep patterns. Remember, most children live in the moment and are limited to putting a situation into perspective with the brief life experiences they have lived through. It is difficult for children to comprehend and frame periods, so their responses and reactions to their new environment should be received with a measure of understanding, as these may be unpredictable to some extent.

Children may not fully appreciate the event's duration, the significance, or the present dangers. With their curiosity brimming, they can crave interaction and activity, and these needs can be tough to meet within the context of an emergency shelter. Unfortunately, predators are a reality; they exist. Providing children the protection they need will include identifying individuals who know precisely how to manipulate a child into a situation that favors their malintent. The responsibility of caring for children in an environment like a shelter is not ideal; meals may be scarce, routines may be disrupted, and strangers will be plentiful. The weight of caring and establishing security for children is a huge one that sits upon the emergency manager's shoulders and the leadership they provide.

Intellectual Disabilities:

Members of the population with mental health issues or developmental disabilities may require additional supervision, resources, and care. Often, these individuals who face mental health disorders and who have developmental disabilities may have difficulty comprehending and applying the new rules and regulations of the shelter they've been permitted to stay within temporarily. Some may not be accustomed to following a daily routine. Others may not fully understand right from wrong in its full capacity and require support and guidance from personnel or friends and family members who are sheltering with them. At times, fellow shelter residents will have their boundaries crossed by individuals with certain disorders unaware of social cues, appropriate behavior, and shared expectations. Given the specific conditions of those with developmental disabilities, it is essential to provide them with protection from predators who may want to take advantage of their vulnerabilities. While physically fully grown, these adults may not have the necessary capabilities and are not mentally developed to the levels expected, based on their age.

Crime:

The sheer variety of criminal activity types found in emergency shelters is not limited to those who have already been convicted of past crimes. In all of its shapes and forms, criminal activity will present itself in a plethora of ways. Crimes will be committed by ordinary people who have found themselves in a stressful situation and are trying to survive a disaster while moving into a shelter. Some come into the shelter already owning nefarious intentions while seeking out methods and opportunities to commit crimes. Most importantly, you have individuals who already possess a known history of past criminal behavior. Because emergencies do not present an ideal timeframe for vetting public members, some public members who possess a known, documented criminal history—including convicted sex offenders—will not be allowed into the shelter under any circumstances, regardless of the circumstances requiring a sheltering situation.

It is of particular importance that you remain vigilant during these crises; crime will happen. Whether these crimes committed are small and petty or major ones, as the emergency manager, it is up to you to set-up a security and support system to minimize crime, alleviate the stress of those under your care, and identify criminal acts before they occur. Be sure not to underestimate minor acts of crime during times of everyday living. These might look isolated to you, but they could become the root and catalyst for creating a hazardous environment within the walls of your shelter. Take someone hoarding toilet paper, food, or supplies, for example. Essential items like these are most often in limited or rationed availability. When even one person decides to take an extra item, they will be subject to theft, and in a shelter, this means one person lacks a necessary good for their daily use. At times, one *petty* act will soon transpire into an assault, a verbal altercation, or other actions. Most people who find themselves tangled up in a messy situation will become befuddled and will surprise even themselves. They're not used to being involved in circumstances such as the ones they face in the present. Many individuals will get caught up in or among behavior they would not typically be associated with the outside of the intense and stressful sheltering situation they now find themselves in.

When placed under significant and prolonged stressful situations, people will revert to Maslow's Hierarchy of Needs every day and fall within the Physiological and Safety levels. They will do what they can to meet their own primary needs and operate in self-preservation's basic human programming. While this continues, you must do what you and your team can to maintain order within the shelter. Include in your regulations that crimes, specifically listed out, will not be acceptable. Make it crystal clear to everyone that acting out a crime will constitute removal from the shelter, possible prosecution for the crimes, and no readmittance. Managing people's perception of the security, personnel, and structure set to provide a crime-free shelter is critical to make known and communicate.

Religious Beliefs:

It is essential to consider your community's religious backgrounds and do the best you can to respect the beliefs and customs they adhere to. While obtaining this knowledge from every single family who walks into your shelter may not be entirely possible, you must know, at a minimum, how your expectations, regulations, and rules relate to or affect family units that honor different religious practices. For example, in some cultures, when speaking to a family, you must address the head of the household directly and not the family as a whole. Anyone outside of the core family cannot speak to a woman directly or physically touch her during a medical situation unless the male counterpart is present. There are situations in shelters and other types of facilities where individuals are offended. To honor their beliefs, they must refuse to do what you ask them to do. For example, women who live in cultures where a headdress must be worn at all times have been forced to remove their headdress when taking a photo for identification purposes. Some officers, unaware of the reason behind their lack of cooperativity, see this objection as refusing to obey orders. In many situations, this confuses language barriers can largely contribute to the frustration and misunderstandings that arise. It is crucial to locate individuals within the shelter, even if they are their children, to act as interpreters for the family. This can significantly help everyone be in sync, better understand each person's religious beliefs and resulting actions while still empowering them. You want to make sure everyone, regardless of their religious beliefs, is respected and honored.

Alcoholics/Drug Abusers:

Alcoholics and drug abusers who join your shelter need to be closely monitored, especially if an individual experiences withdrawal or delirium tremens (the DTs). Trained personnel will be a considerable asset in monitoring such individuals and knowing what signs to look for if this occurs. Also, be aware that those with addiction issues often use private areas, such as locked restrooms, to inject drugs or consume alcohol. Since children tend to explore and play and hide in different areas frequently, there's a chance they will run into needles or drug packaging left behind. Dedicated shelter staff who take these individuals under their wings during their shelter stay must be able to build strong rapport and keep high traffic zones clean, sanitized, and hazardous-free for the scores of people, especially young children, who will be continually passing through these areas.

Visual/Hearing Impaired:

You should be aware of individuals who have partial hearing or visual impairments, including those who are completely deaf or blind. Usually, these individuals are familiar with their impairments or have somebody to help them navigate their daily activities. However, I have found that both of these may not always be the case in an emergency. Even for those who have learned to adapt to life with their impairments, being in an emergency shelter can be overwhelming. Orientations and helpful personnel will support these individuals as they try to settle into their new environment. They will also need superior protection from those around them who may seek to exploit them due to their disabilities. It is a good idea to have materials, such as literature or pictures, that can help your communication with these individuals readily available—specifically for the hearing impaired—and have a sign language interpreter available to assist with communication through an online platform Zoom or Skype. Attention for those living with impairments is vital to helping everyone's stay in the shelter become the most convenient and pleasant one possible.

Severe and obvious medical conditions or symptoms of the disease:

Individuals with apparent signs and symptoms of medical conditions, injury, or possibly infectious diseases need to be diverted to a hospital setting immediately. Prepare the transportation to be made available or arranged beforehand. Hence, there are zero delays in transporting these people out of the shelter and into a clinic or hospital, where their conditions can be appropriately assessed and treated. Some ideas for setting up the transportation include the use of school buses, church vans, or ambulances on stand-by at the shelter to provide both on-site professional care of small medical issues and quick transport.

Mobility Issues:

When addressing the needs of disabled or mobility-impaired individuals, you need to have a plan for where you will strategically place these members of the population. The elderly and those with mobility issues should be housed closest to the restrooms, and adjacent to a wall or corner of the floorplan, to limit the amount of foot traffic walking through their area. Remember, some crimes that happened would not have happened if the opportunity didn't present itself. Using the set-up and existing features of the shelter building will help protect these individuals, make life much easier for them with fewer travel distances, and increase their security and safety levels.

Deceased:

This is an unfortunate reality during an emergency sheltering situation; some people's lives will end as they stay in a shelter for various reasons. You must have a plan in place with the medical examiner's office to arrange the storage, transportation, and notification of the deceased's families. You will also need to be prepared to address large audiences about the deceased individual's state or status and their whereabouts without violating the Health Insurance Portability and Accountability Act (HIPAA). Get very familiar with HIPAA if you are not already— you will thank me for it. Save yourself from some dicey legal situations that could have (and should have) been avoided and learn the ins and outs of HIPAA to know its guidelines better and to be prepared.

★★★★

CHAPTER 12

SHELTERING ISSUES

YOUR PLANNING SHOULD INCLUDE SOLUTIONS FOR:

A Lack of Security:

Consider all of your available options to provide a high level of security within your shelter. Seek out potential staff, including sworn and unsworn officers, private security, vetted volunteers, church members, and individuals from civic organizations.

Rules and Regulations:

The documents outlining specific shelter rules and regulations need to be complete. Any delays in having this ready will delay providing the communication, structure, guidance, and organization for those occupying the shelter. Outline all of the significant and fundamental expectations everyone under the shelter's roof is required to follow and relay all of the consequences for failing to adhere to any of them. All prohibited items, behaviors, and conduct needs to be posted in clear, familiar, and visible locations, with legible print.

Exposure to Predators:

One of the "open sources" (meaning openly available to the public) of intelligence gathering is being aware of items that must be done well in advance of an emergency event. The importance of keeping up with available information on a routine basis is the following of local crime *blotters* and the public posting of convicted registered and known unregistered sex offenders on your shelter information board. This critical information should also be posted in the restrooms, at the shelter entrance, and all the building exits.

<u>This Serves Several Purposes:</u>

1. It shows you are serious about the security of the shelter inhabitants.
2. It demonstrates you are aware and prepared to deal with an encounter.
3. Posting the pictures or mugshots may serve as a deterrent to offenders attempting to gain entry.
4. This will help obtain and uphold a trespassing charge if someone is found past the shelter's entry point.

Exposure to Criminals:

Make sure you have a police liaison or a sheriff's deputy detailed to your shelter. Even with their presence, you still need to be familiar with local known criminals, and what kinds of illegal activities happen most frequently in your community. This will help you when planning and arranging your security team's assembly, mainly if the actionable items include acquiring items your team will need to operate effectively. Examples of equipment necessary include locks, lockable filing cabinets for belongings and medications, prepared handouts educating people about common shelter crimes, and avoiding shelter crimes.

Money, Medication, and Jewelry:

One of the most significant contributors to opportunity crimes is personal belongings, significant cash, medication, or jewelry left out in others' open and straightforward views. At a minimum, you should have on-hand large, non-sealing envelopes that can be opened and closed for individuals to place their personal belongings in. These envelopes should have the owner's name and a copy of their driver's license or I.D. attached to the outside, along with an inventory list of contents. Another copy of the I.D. should be placed inside the envelope for safekeeping, so the owner can be easily identified when retrieving the item. Shelter teams can track these items in a secure location. If available, a lockable filing cabinet should also be accessible for everyone to secure their jewelry, cash, or medications safely. Everyday activities, such as restroom use, leave the elderly and disabled open to the theft of their medications and belongings. It is of great importance to place safety and security at the top of your to-do list and not neglect it for smaller, everyday activities that expose vulnerable special populations to petty crime.

★★★★

Special populations may require a significant concentration of limited resources. Remember that running a shelter is the ultimate multi-tasking endeavor. It is also a logistical nightmare for resources and supplies. Every time you are delayed by dealing with one issue, ten more are brewing in the background. Unfortunately, this means that some of the basic things, including creature comforts, may go by-the-wayside. One way to avoid stretching resources too thin is to group high-needs populations with the best you can. For example, suppose medical attention is being used for the elderly and the disabled continuously. In that case, it may make sense to house them close to each other within the shelter and house individuals—such as families with children requiring special medical care, diabetics, or other chronic illnesses with them. Members of special populations may have limited mobility, hearing, vision, or mental health issues, which may not allow them to function appropriately in a mixed and unfamiliar environment.

★★★★

Special populations may require <u>constant supervision</u> since they are more likely to fall victim to:

- They are being preyed upon by people *willing* to help them.
- Increased chances of significant injury or death.
- Increased chances of abandonment by family.
- Increased exposure to public health issues.
- Increased issues with maintaining proper hygiene.
- Lack of proper dietary needs, available alternatives, or special preparation needs.

CONCLUSION

Almost all of the issues you will face during an emergency or disaster event can be mitigated beforehand. I think you know what I'm talking about during that long period when nothing was going on for weeks. You thought the job was easy; this is when you have ample time to plan for a disaster and run a shelter. The moment you finally get a break from the monotony of meetings, complaints, and training is the perfect time for you to solidify preparations, so managing a shelter with special populations after a disaster can go much more seamlessly and smoothly.

I cannot stress enough to be even more proactive during this downtime on the job. If you are set up to be solely reactive in your position, you will fail and fail miserably. If you find yourself with nothing to do, you are already in the wrong. Period. For those of you who already have plans in place, I implore you to go back and make them better. Test your plans, own your mistakes, and fix the issues. President John F. Kennedy said it best: "Victory has a thousand fathers, but defeat is an orphan." In my experience, I do not believe a more accurate or true statement was ever uttered.

★★★★

So, how do we mitigate a majority of these problems before we ever have to deal with them? I think all of the topics covered in previous chapters will give you some groundwork and insight to, at the very least, begin building your road map to success. This book isn't written purely based on my personal opinions, but rather, it is based on the wisdom I have acquired over a long career in emergency services. You won't avoid all of the issues that arise throughout your career, but at least you will be familiar with some valuable knowledge and be better prepared to deal with what lies ahead. When your community presents its particular circumstance to solve, you, too, will gain wisdom through adversity, make mistakes along the way, and be even more ready for the next emergency that comes along to challenge you.

★★★★

ABOUT THE AUTHOR

Brian K. Rand has served the United States and its citizens for over 20 years in public service. Brian also worked privately as a trusted risk advisor executive. He is a graduate of Anna Maria College in Paxton, MA, with a master's degree in Public Administration and Emergency Management, a bachelor's degree in Fire Science Administration (Summa Cum Laude) from Salem State University in Salem, MA, and an associate's degree in Fire Protection and Safety Technology (Summa Cum Laude) from Middlesex Community College in Bedford, MA.

After serving as a U.S. Marine Infantry Sergeant assigned to and deploying with, the First Fleet Antiterrorism Security Team (USMC FAST Co.), Brian worked as a fire officer for Metro Boston, Watertown Fire Department and served as the Department Emergency Medical Services (EMS) Coordinator, Training Officer, Infection Control Officer, and Emergency Management Coordinator. Reenlisting as a U.S. Army Combat Medic during his fire department career, Brian again served the citizens of the United States working with burn and blast victims of improvised explosive devices (IEDs), rocket-propelled grenades (RPGs), and other various combat-related burn injuries at the Brook Army Medical Hospital in San Antonio, TX.

Brian served as an awarded Intelligence Officer and subject matter expert (SME) in emergency management and preparedness specializing in chemical, biological, radiological, nuclear, and high-yield explosions (CBRNE), improvised explosives device expert, and mass casualty incident planner for the Intelligence Community (IC) and the Department of Defense.

Brian was hired as a multi-state Director for Pinkerton© Corporate Risk Management. Based from

Washington D.C. and covering Maryland, Delaware, and Philadelphia field offices, Brian provided comprehensive risk management and full-spectrum private security services to over 90-percent of all Fortune 1000 companies in over 100 counties.

AWARDS

- The United States Presidential award of *"Champion of Change"* presented by **President Barack Obama**
- The FEMA *"Community Preparedness Hero"* award presented by **Craig Fugate**, Administrator of FEMA
- **(5)** Five awards from the Department of Defense and the Intelligence Community (IC)
- **(2)** Two awards for the preservation of human life from the Metro Boston, Watertown, MA Fire Department
- The USMC Scholastic Excellence Award

REFERENCES

1. aljazeera.com/news/2020/9/14/which-countries-have-not-reported-any-coronavirus-cases; web 2020
2. jennynovak.com/2020/04/who-are-em/; web 2020
3. govtech.com/page-not-foundr=&keywords=em%2520emergency-blogs%2520managing-crisis%2520characteristics-of-effective-emergency-managers-part-2.html 2020/; web 2020
4. work.chron.com/duties-emergency-managers-12209.html/; web 2020
5. uasem.org/what-is-emergency-management/; web 2020
6. bls.gov/ooh/management/emergency-management-directors.htm/; web 2020
7. govtech.com/ =em+emergency-blogs+managing-crisis+characteristics-of-effective-emergency-managers-part-1.html/; web 2020
8. domesticpreparedness.com/commentary/the-seven-and-a-half-traits-of-the-ultimate-emergency-manager//; web 2020
9. rollingstone.com/culture/culture-features/CHOP-CHAZ-seattle-autonomous-zone-inside-protests-1017637//; web 2020
10. thecut.com/2020/07/whats-going-on-in-CHAZ-the-seattle-autonomous-zone.html/; web 2020
11. thecut.com/2020/07/whats-going-on-in-CHAZ-the-seattle-autonomous-zone.html/; web 2020
12. nytimes.com/2020/07/01/us/seattle-protest-zone-CHOP-CHAZ-unrest.html/; web 2020
13. archive.curbed.com/2020/6/23/21300240/CHAZ-CHOP-seattle-autonomous-zone-stories/; web 2020
14. cnn.com/2020/06/24/us/seattle-autonomous-zone-protesters-leaving/index.html/; web 2020
15. dictionary.com/browse/too-many-cooks-spoil-the-broth/; web 2020
16. nationalservice.gov/sites/default/files/olc/moodle/ds_online_orientation/viewf265.html?id=3139&chapterid=908/; web 2020
17. investopedia.com/terms/o/organizational-structure.asp%5c/; web 2020

18. cato.org/blog/hurricane-katrina-remembering-federal-failures/; web 2020

19. nationalgeographic.com/environment/natural-disasters/reference/hurricane-katrina/#close 2020/; web 2020

20. usnews.com/news/the-report/articles/2015/08/28/hurricane-katrina-was-the-beginning-of-the-end-for-george-w-bush/; web 2020

21. nytimes.com/2005/09/05/us/nationalspecial/after-failures-government-officials-play-blame-game.html/; web 2020

22. nationalgeographic.com/environment/natural-disasters/reference/hurricane-katrina/#close/; web 2020

23. nytimes.com/2013/03/15/us/gov-rick-snyder-kevyn-orr-emergency-manager-detroit.html/; web 2020

24. typeinvestigations.org/investigation/2020/07/09/domestic-terror-in-the-age-of-trump//; web 2020

25. newamerica.org/in-depth/terrorism-in-america/what-threat-united-states-today//; web 2020

26. washingtonpost.com/national-security/domestic-terror--particularly-white-supremacist-violence--as-big-a-threat-as-isis-al-qaeda-dhs-says/2019/09/20/dff8aa4e-dbad-11e9-bfb1-849887369476_story.html/; web 2020

27. everycrsreport.com/reports/R44921.html#_Toc491092788/; web 2020

28. nytimes.com/article/what-ANTIFA-trump.html/; web 2020

29. politicaldictionary.com/words/plausible-deniability//; web 2020

30. wbez.org/stories/history-of-violence-chicago-during-the-capone-era-and-today/6bff3ad9-097a-42e8-ac23-bc90d83d5bdb/; web 2020

31. ourworldindata.org/terrorism/; web 2020

32. washingtonpost.com/politics/buildings-burn-and-trump-talks-tough-where-are-the-healers/2020/05/30/437cd1e0-a27c-11ea-9590-1858a893bd59_story.html/; web 2020

33. cnn.com/2019/08/07/politics/white-house-domestic-terrorism/index.html/; web 2020

34. indian.senate.gov/news/press-release/hoeven-senate-passes-bill-repealing-obsolete-indian-laws/; web 2020

35. reason.com/2020/02/05/government-should-repeal-out-of-date-laws//; web 2020

36. goodhousekeeping.com/life/news/g4039/crazy-state-laws/?slide=42/; web 2020

37. nytimes.com/2020/03/31/us/politics/coronavirus-defense-production-act.html/; web 2020

38. techcrunch.com/2020/04/17/gm-delivers-first-ventilators-under-30000-unit-government-contract//; web 2020

39. theatlantic.com/ideas/archive/2020/06/how-actually-fix-americas-police/612520//; web 2020

40. illinoispolicy.org/what-powers-does-pritzker-have-in-an-emergency-and-what-has-he-ordered-so-far//; web 2020

41. latimes.com/archives/la-xpm-2005-dec-06-na-commish6-story.html/; web 2020

42. latimes.com/nation/la-xpm-2011-aug-30-la-na-911-report-card-20110831-story.html/; web 2020

43. training.fema.gov/emiweb/downloads/is111_unit%204.pdf/; web 2020

44. bloomberg.com/news/articles/2020-02-10/the-shrinking-of-u-s-household-size-may-be-coming-to-an-end?sref=O57BN56n/; web 2020

45. International Association of Police Chiefs: Leadership in Police Services (1990) Print.

46. verywellmind.com/what-is-maslows-hierarchy-of-needs-4136760/; web 2020

47. mindtools.com/pages/article/newLDR_86.htm#:~:text=Team%20formation%20usually%20follows%20easily,adjourning%22%20or%20%20%22mourning.%22/; web 2020

48. thezebra.com/insurance-news/4674/emergency-preparedness-seniors-disabled//; web 2020

49. todaysgeriatricmedicine.com/news/ex_082809_01.shtml/; web 2020

50. caninejournal.com/disaster-preparedness-for-pets//; web 2020

51. thehill.com/changing-america/opinion/494284-isolated-with-no-family-members-for-non-english-speakers-with/; web 2020

52. translate.google.com/?ui=tob/; web 2020

53. reuters.com/article/us-health-translations/google-translate-mostly-accurate-in-test-with-patient-instructions-idUSKCN1QE2KB/; web 2020

54. nytimes.com/2020/09/25/parenting/disaster-evacuation-kids-coping.html/; web 2020

www.ingramcontent.com/pod-product-compliance
Lightning Source LLC
Chambersburg PA
CBHW040124270326
41926CB00001B/1